It's Not About the Activity

Thinking Outside the Toolbox in Equine-Facilitated Psychotherapy and Learning

Veronica Lac, PhD

University
PROFESSORS PRESS

www.univeristyprofessorspress.com
Colorado Springs, CO

First Published in 2020, University Professors Press.

Print ISBN: 978-1-939686-59-6
ebook ISBN: 978-1-939686-60-2

University Professors Press
Colorado Springs, CO
www.universityprofessorspress.com

Front Cover Art by Kelsey Walne Photography
Cover Design by Laura Ross

With themes central to the human experience, Veronica Lac's new book highlights relationships, meaning, and embodied experiences in facilitated interactions with horses. She braids philosophy, inclusivity, and personal narrative along with case studies that are not about the activity. Lac has created a needed and much welcomed resource for those who want to include horses in their services.

Nina Ekholm Fry, Director of Equine Programs
Institute for Human-Animal Connection, University of Denver

Veronica has written an amazing companion to her first book! *It's Not About the Activity* is immediately useful, with important ideas in succinct, bite-sized chapters. The Foundations section articulates the theory of growth and change, and how to help others achieve them with horses. I'm really grateful for the lucid and simple distinction between Equine-Facilitated Psychotherapy and Equine-Facilitated Learning! The Applications section is a great reference point for those seeking structure in their practice, without "one-size-fits-all" limitations. The Case Studies bring it all together, demonstrating theory in practice. Thank you so much, Veronica!"

Shannon Knapp, MA, NLC-EAP & Trainer
Author of *More than a Mirror: Horses, Humans and Therapeutic Practice* and
Horse Sense Business Sense: Starting your own Equine Assisted Program

Veronica is incredibly skilled at holding the balance between structure and process. She encourages readers to think beyond activities and to focus on the relationship that is unfolding between horse and client. This book also provides one of the clearest delineations I've seen between equine-facilitated learning and equine-facilitated psycho-therapy with practical steps to demystify program development and session planning and case examples for each scope of practice. A valuable resource regardless of your primary approach to facilitating horse-human interactions.

Sarah Schlote, MA, Founder of EQUUSOMA®
Horse-Human Trauma Recovery

This book was an absolute delight to read. Chock full of ethics, scope of practice, principles, theory and philosophy, and, importantly, specific examples, interventions, and case studies. This is such a rich resource for all equine assisted/facilitated students and practitioners to deep dive into the HERD model—a relational, ethical and professional approach founded by author Veronica Lac.

The book title itself pinpoints such an important topic in the equine assisted/facilitated field as it encourages students and practitioners to reflect on 'what is this work really about at its core?' When I hear people ask for a list of activities with horses, I fear they have not had the opportunity to understand what equine assisted/facilitated practice is really about: awareness in relationship. This book begins to address this issue head-on from the HERD perspective. It is indeed a sad day when horses are used as activities or metaphors for humans to learn, grow, and heal—for both the humans (who are unaware of what is missing) and the horses (who are objectified, with good intentions, perhaps). Similarly, there is a new trend in the field to include "certified therapy horses" (and "certified therapy animals"), rather than actually training and certifying the practitioner! Quick fixes and appearances of best practice cannot replace substantial training, supervision, and qualification in the animal assisted/facilitated field. *It's Not About the Activity* introduces readers to the depth of what equine assisted/facilitated work can include and gives diverse case studies to illustrate the HERD process. Thank you, Veronica!

Meg Kirby, Founder of The Equine Psychotherapy Institute
and Animal Assisted Psychotherapy Institute,
Mental Health Social Worker
and Gestalt Psychotherapist of 23 years

I truly loved every page of this book—going back repeatedly until I was sure I'd grasped each concept and could apply it. No other book on this subject demonstrates the complexity and depth of skill required by an Equine-Facilitated Psychotherapy and Equine-Facilitated Learning practitioner. It seamlessly combines the science, philosophy, psychology, relationships, and personal inner work that every practitioner needs to understand in order to do this work safely. Every practitioner should buy this book, devour it over and over again, and continue to deepen their own process in service of both horses and humans.

Jude Jennison, Founder of Leaders by Nature
and Author of *Leading Through Uncertainty*

Dedication

For Reba, the chestnut mare that turned my world around and upside down. As the heart of my herd, your love and presence have shown me who I have longed to be. Every day you help make my dreams come true simply by being you. You are in my heart always, and I am forever grateful.

Table of Contents

Acknowledgments

Bringing a book to life is not a solo journey. While the act of writing can be isolating, it requires the support of those around me to hold space for birthing a new creation. I experience my time spent sequestered on my farm, foregoing social events and other pursuits, in an effort to bring words to a page, tortuous at worst or a process of metamorphosis at best. For me, neither occurs without high levels of angst, doubt, and mountains of Cheetos.

I am deeply grateful to my husband, Quan, for indulging me in my passions, patiently awaiting the completion of whatever new project I dive into, encouraging me to reach for my dreams and holding my hand to steady me when I wobble. Leaving behind his dream of living in the hustle and bustle of city life and joining me in an adventure of living a farm life has not been without sacrifice. Every milestone reached has not been achieved alone but shared equally with him by my side.

I am thankful to Sarah Morehouse, who trusted in my vision enough to move across state lines to work alongside me. The smooth running of The HERD Institute® is entirely down to her hard work and dedication to details that I cannot fathom. The freedom that exists for me to travel to worldwide engagements would not be possible without her support. As "godmother" to all my animals, Sarah has been entrusted with everything I hold dear, and I have been forever changed by her faith in me.

Elisabeth Crabtree, Alison McCabe, Chris Goodall, and Catherine Frend Gillihan have all been instrumental in the growth of the HERD. I am thankful for their love, guidance, friendship, and honest feedback in ways to continuously improve what we offer as a faculty team. They make my journey as a reluctant business leader so much less daunting.

I have been so privileged to have met some fellow teachers in this field who have supported me on my journey. Barbara Rector is a woman of grace and wisdom, whose presence soothes my soul, and I am blessed to call her a friend and mentor. Meg Kirby, founder and director of the Equine Psychotherapy Institute in Australia, and Sarah Schlote, creator of EQUUSOMA®, have been solid sounding boards for me as we each step more boldly into this field. The sense of sisterhood I feel in connection with them leaves my nerdy brain and geeky heart jumping for joy.

My heart fills with love and gratitude as I think of each and every single student and graduate who has joined the HERD programs. With every iteration of the curricula, and every time I teach, I learn something new. I am so proud of the community that we are building together and thankful for how each member of the HERD shows up to support one another. I am truly humbled by their talents and their passion for what they bring to the communities they serve.

Finally, I am beyond grateful for all the animals in my life who inspire me to do this work. To our dog, Alfie, whose aging body reminds me that time is precious, encouraging me to slow down and be present with him, I offer my continued devotion. To Tyson, who reaffirms my faith that love can change anything, I will always have room on my pillow. To Carly, my cat who joins in with every session I lead, and to my chickens who bring so much laughter to my life, I promise to keep you safe. To my equine herds, past and present, I profess my heartfelt gratitude: Rupert, Reba, Cheyenne, Arrow, Infinity, Tess, Lucinda, Spirit, Samson, and so many more; I thank them all for leading me home.

Veronica Lac, PhD
The HERD Institute®

Foreword

While Dr. Veronica Lac's first book, *Equine-Facilitated Psychotherapy & Learning: The Human–Equine Relational Development (HERD) Approach,* is a must-read text for every clinician offering psychotherapy with the help of horses and program directors seeking knowledge of Equine-Facilitated Psychotherapy & Learning (EFPL), this second book is a stunning explanation of principles and practices taught by The Human–Equine Relational Development (HERD) Institute. This extremely valuable teaching text is essential for clinical EFP practitioners, EFL educators, coaches, instructors, and those program organizers and development staff seeking clarity regarding the distinctions between EFP and EFL.

For the aspiring student and practitioner of wellness work with horses, Veronica offers sensible and practical assessments in essential considerations that include:

- Knowing yourself, and the importance of making learning about yourself a lifelong practice
- Knowing your horses
- Knowing your personal philosophy and beliefs
- Knowing and practicing your core values
- Treating your human staff with warm regard
- Being prepared to abandon your plan and go with what is emerging relationally between your client/participants and the horse(s)

I would add, approaching all in your realm, both two and four legged, with warm regard, and offering specific praise often.

I loved reading this book! I view it as a precise summary of my life's work teaching and learning Adventures in Awareness. Veronica's rendition of the significance of "being with" is very powerful, rooted as it is in congruence. This matching of an individual's interior landscape with outward expression is essential for connected heart bonding with horses, and with others. Her entire text serves as a descriptive explanation and rationale behind our (Alden, Baldwin, & Rector) nine years of research examining the physiological changes in the human when engaged in professionally facilitated interactions with horses (in groundwork or mounted work).

Veronica's remarkably illuminating case studies in both EFL and EFP demonstrate the essential nature of conscious, continuous knowing and learning about one's self. Adeptness with this skill and its practice is necessary for an intimate, trusting relationship with another being—human, equine, dog, cat, bird, or other species. Indeed, skill in being congruent—matching your interior thoughts, feelings, and emotions, with your outward expression of facial cues, body language, and behaviors—produces coherence. Veronica offers a phenomenological method, which I know as "bookmarking," for later self-reflection that consciously sets aside the practitioner's awareness of a disconnect in themselves in favor of that of the clients or participants.

The state of coherence is associated in the human with a high degree of effective function. Think of Simone Biles in her stupendous floor exercise performance at the Olympics. Her seemingly easy "in the flow" athletic movement exemplifies congruent coherence. As she closed her eyes a moment and took a deep breath, I experienced it as a moment where she knew "she had this," followed by a flawless, seemingly easy execution. Or, cast your mind's eye back to Captain Sullenberger piloting his US Airways flight over the Hudson Bridge into a successful "all on board safe" water landing. I credit the moment he turned to his co-pilot to affirm they had tried all they knew from the checklist as he told air traffic control they would be in the Hudson and received the response, "I'll call the boats." At that moment, what I know as the Universal Field of Intelligence and Awareness lined up to place all involved in Flow. An effective safe landing resulted.

Flow is a non-ordinary state of consciousness resulting from coherence, a skill acquired with practice of congruence, and easy to learn with the help of horses. The process grows out of recognizing the Mirror our horses present. I do not mean mirror as an object, the shiny surface you look into to view your external appearance. No, I mean mirror as a verb—a direct expression of an individual's interior landscape as *responded* to by the horse(s).

The activity of consciously looking inside one's self to view a clear picture of one's interior landscape is Psyche at work. Do one's internal thoughts, feelings, and emotions (conscious or unconscious) match one's external outward appearance of facial expressions, body posture, and way of moving and behaving? It is this internal process that the horses respond to from a heart-centered space. Our heart's physiology is felt by the horses even prior to our physical appearance in their space.

The initiation of dawning awareness by our research teams' measures and technology of this process began in 2013, with our initial pilot study at Ann Alden's Borderlands center in Sonoita, Arizona. I believe a contributing factor for myself and Ann Alden was our experience earlier in the year with Holly, the rescued wild, untamed baby zebra living and teaching with Jackie Stevenson's Pebble Lodge herd in Novelty, Ohio. This was also when I first met Veronica. The account of Holly volunteering for an Adventures in Awareness Invitational Approach demonstration of working with elderly people, in front of 80 global participants at the European Association of Horse Assisted Education, is available elsewhere and included in my own, currently a work in progress, second book.

Yes, this work is not about the activity, and all about relationships! This principle works for all in our lives. Happy reading. Treat yourself to several visits, for this is a remarkable book.

Heart Hugs,

Barbara K. Rector
February 2020
Skyview Casita
www.adventuresinawareness.net

Part 1

Foundations

Chapter 1

An Introduction and a Disclaimer

"So what activity should I do with them?"

Those of us in the field of training practitioners in the art of Equine-Facilitated Psychotherapy and Learning will recognize that this is the question that we hear most often. Particularly for beginning practitioners, the idea of not having something set up and ready, or a set plan to follow for a session, creates anxiety. We live in a results-driven and evidence-based world where treatment plans and organizational goals are often prioritized over embodied experiential healing and learning. As trainers and practitioners in this field, it is easy to become pulled into these expectations to provide tangible, replicable, and workbook-based approaches to working with our students and participants. The assumption is that if you can replicate something, then it is of value, and deemed to be effective. The belief is that if you have a workbook to follow, then students will have something to measure themselves against and know if they've done it right. The idea of having a toolbox of activities to delve into suggests that it is the activity that facilitates the healing and learning.

This book challenges this paradigm. This book also challenges practitioners to evaluate their foundational principles of what it means to partner with our equine colleagues and question the value of "set piece" activities. I am referring here to the countless creative but well-worn activities that are used within equine-facilitated work, with set guidelines on how to run them. While having some structure in place for a session is useful, creating standardized processes in the form of step-by-step activities takes us away from the healing and learning that horses offer.

Within the equine-facilitated industry, we pride ourselves on harnessing the power of equine wisdom, trusting that their generous hearts will pull us in and open us up, and in doing so offer insight and healing to our clients and participants. We espouse the relational quality of this modality, claiming that it is authentic encounters within this unique environment that allow our participants to translate what they have learned into their everyday lives. So, if this is true—and I wholeheartedly believe that it is—then why do we focus so much on the need to follow an agenda with set activities in sessions?

Following a predetermined agenda for a session is representative of the medical model approach to mental health as well as the need for certainty in a commercialized world. The pressure to deliver something tangible, measurable, and cost effective drives us to offer set-piece activities that allow us to join the dots for clients so that they feel like they have achieved something. It also allows us to feel like we have accomplished something more concrete. But something is lost in that process— something that is fundamental in any transformational endeavor, that is precious, profound, and personal. That something? Meaning.

How often have you encountered an experience where you were certain that an individual would react in a particular way, only to be surprised by the outcome? Whether this is in a professional or personal setting, there may be innumerable moments where your perception of an experience is vastly different to someone else's. By embracing this process as an organic and essential way of being with our horses and participants, it allows us to be guided by our participants' perceptions, thereby not only providing us with a deeper understanding of their experience of the interactions with the horses, but more important, giving *them* the opportunity to explore how those interactions can shift their understanding and experience of themselves.

This approach to healing and learning is influenced by the existential–humanistic and Gestalt therapy trainings that form the bedrock of my way of being with others. This book will offer readers some insight into these foundational principles within the context of equine-facilitated work. In doing so, practitioners can become more confident in the meaningful experiences that they offer by meeting clients and participants authentically, rather than following a routine progression of activities. By attending to the needs of the client populations that we serve, and really understanding them, we can create powerful and transformative experiences in partnership with our horses.

I want to be clear that I am not advocating for the removal of props, games, and activities from the arena. Rather, the purpose of this book is to demonstrate the powerful impact of allowing for a more creative and co-constructed version of these activities to emerge in the moment with the people we serve and the horses we partner with; it is a rallying call to let go of structure in order to step into the flow of what might be. It is a reminder that it is in those moments when we can step back to hold the space between humans and horses, and allow the relationships to unfold, that we are truly facilitating healing and learning.

Chapter 2

Learning to Be Me

As a therapist, my core training came from a Gestalt psychotherapy tradition. I later broadened this perspective through my PhD program in Existential–Humanistic and Transpersonal Psychology. These are mostly fancy words for the "simple" endeavor of discovering human potential within relationships. One of my favorite concepts within Gestalt theory is what's known as the Paradoxical Theory of Change. Arnold Beisser, [1] an American psychiatrist, proposed that change occurs not when we are trying to become someone else but when we accept and claim more of who we already are. I love this because it feels to me like the ultimate offering of self-compassion and optimism. The idea that I—in the form of this existential, angst-filled, anxiety laden, and uncertain being—can change, develop, and reach a higher potential simply by accepting who I already am feels so hopeful and soothing. Instead of striving to be someone I'm not, pretending to appear other than I am, and/or dismissing myself in the process, I can give myself permission to be as I am, in all of who I am? What a relief! Even as I write this, I can hear and feel the rousing chorus of the anthem "This is me" from the movie *The Greatest Showman,*[2] coursing through my body.

> *I am brave, I am bruised.*
> *I am who I'm meant to be*
> *This is me!*

Of course, in reality, the process of accepting who we are, as we are, cannot be achieved simply through singing our greatest anthems, whatever secret fantasies I might have about musical theater, and our struggles continue despite our intellectual knowing of this theory. What we need in those moments is a hand to hold, a push in the right direction, or a word of encouragement from someone else. Within an equine-facilitated setting, the skill of the facilitator or therapist comes into play in these moments. How can we support our clients and participants to step outside of what they have habitually experienced within relationships, and explore a different way of being with others, while staying true to themselves?

It is in these moments where another Gestalt theory can support the process. Joseph Zinker,[3] a renowned Gestalt therapist, viewed the therapeutic process as a space to allow clients to try out new ways of being in relationships. He suggested that the relationship between the client and therapist is a fluid, creative, work in progress that allows space for experimentation in order to improvise, invent, and co-create experiences of connection or disconnection. This supports an individual to translate these new ways of being into their everyday lives. I believe that working with horses enhances this process of experimentation, allowing clients and participants to find authentic ways of relating in their interactions with the horses and integrating these experiences into their lives.

When working in an equine-facilitated setting, I hold this frame of reference in mind, trusting that as I bring myself authentically into the process that it will allow others to do the same.

Chapter 3

The HERD Approach

The Importance of Language

The HERD approach holds the core belief that growth and learning are optimized through authentic relationships. This means acknowledging that everyone in the group/team is a sentient being with their own thoughts and feelings that are equally important. This includes the horses. So if we are to subscribe to this way of working, we need to be consistent in our use of language to reflect this process.

Through the years, I have heard people within the equine-facilitated industry talk about "using" horses in a therapy or learning setting. I want to be clear that this does not sit well with me and goes against everything that The HERD Institute® stands for. Saying that we "use" our horses not only positions them in a subservient position but also objectifies them, turning them into tools rather than living, breathing beings. This may sound picky to some people, but I believe that it is important to be consistent in upholding our principle beliefs, and the language we use makes an impact on the people we serve. Do we want our clients and participants to think about the horses as a tool? Or do we want to encourage and support the building of a relationship with our horses as unique contributors to the process?

At The HERD Institute, we talk about partnering or working with our horses as co-facilitators of the equine-facilitated session, whether this is in the context of learning or psychotherapy. We give them equal standing as valued members of the facilitation team. After all, they are the reason we work in this way; without them, what are we providing? I want to acknowledge the commitment we can make to them to honor their contributions to the work that we do, beginning with the language we use.

Language sets the scene for your participants in a number of ways. When working with vulnerable populations, it is important to remember to use person-first language. In the same way as our not wanting to objectify the horses, we do not want to pathologize our participants. What I mean by this is that we need to be mindful of not reducing our participants to their diagnoses. For example, referring to people who use wheelchairs, versus the wheelchair-bound; participants with eating disorders, versus the anorexic client; a child from an abusive family, versus the battered child. Person-first language allows us to focus on the individual rather than their diagnosis or symptom. Not only does this support the participant to experience themselves as more than their struggles or condition, it also helps us to see them more clearly as individuals in their own right. Of course, this attitude needs to be extended to our equine partners too.

In this way, we can set the scene for an inclusive space as we meet our participants. Here, the language emphasized is the use of the term "we." We, meaning everyone who is present—including the horses, participants, and facilitators—are meeting to begin a journey together. By referring to the group as we, us, and our, rather then you and your, we bring ourselves into the group as part of the experience, and participants can feel a more solid sense of belonging to the process.

Distinctions Between Client and Participant

You may have noticed that I have been referring to the people we serve as "clients or participants." This is a deliberate distinction. When I use the term "clients," I am referring to either the counseling or psychotherapy client (I don't like the more medicalized version of "patient") or the organization/person who is paying for your services. Within an equine-facilitated learning context, I refer to the people who are attending the session as "participants."

The reason for this distinction? In order to provide a safe and successful program, the first question needs to be "Who is my client?" This may seem obvious, but in reality, the "client" may not be the person who is attending the session. So, from that point of view, we really need to assess whether the client's goals are aligned with the participants' goals. For example, if you are designing a program for at-risk youth, and you're talking to a local high school, your "client" and the funding source of the program may be the school. Your participants, the at-risk youth, may not be part of the conversation. Similarly, if you're speaking to the human resources director of a company that is interested in setting up a corporate teambuilding event for the finance department, your client is not your participant. In contrast, in a psychotherapy context, your client is usually the person coming to you for therapy, and your focus is geared towards the presenting issues that emerge in your initial assessments. Having said that, there will also be instances where you will have a business client relationship with the referral agency. For example, when I partnered with an eating disorder clinic, my business client was the executive director of the clinic, and my therapy clients were the individuals who were referred to me for sessions. These language distinctions help us to orient towards a more relational way of approaching both the humans and horses that we work with and support us to be more congruent with the philosophy and theory that we practice.

The HERD Models

In my first book,[1] I detailed the philosophical and theoretical principles behind the Human–Equine Relational Development (HERD) Models for Equine-Facilitated Psychotherapy and Learning. These came about as a result of the research I conducted as part of my doctoral program. In the three years since its publication, I have come to an even deeper appreciation for how important it is to have a coherent philosophical base for our approach to this work.

At The HERD Institute®, we believe that the skills required for working in Equine-Facilitated Psychotherapy (EFP) are distinct from those needed in an Equine-Facilitated Learning (EFL) environment. Many people new to this field often position the two domains as EFP being "more/better than" EFL. I want to clarify that, in my view, this is simply not true. It is a false comparison, as there are clear differences in aims and objectives, and scope of practice. For this reason, The HERD Institute® offers two separate certification tracks to emphasize the different skills needed in each training program, based on two different models.

What is Scope of Practice?

The key question in working within your scope of practice is this: "Am I providing a service that is legally and ethically within my area of expertise?" In other words, are you a licensed mental health professional (e.g. social worker, marriage and family therapist, psychologist, or counselor)? If so, you would be legally and ethically supported to offer Equine-Facilitated Psychotherapy. If not, you would fall under the scope of practice for Equine-Facilitated Learning. This would include those of you who are qualified as educators, coaches, equine professionals, and therapeutic riding instructors. It's important to note that maintaining scope of practice works both ways because we are not positioning that EFP is "more than" EFL, but that they are different. Leif Hallberg,[2] author of *Walking the Way of the Horse*, suggests that it is the ethical responsibility of the practitioner to be clear about the services they are offering and their scope of practice.

> In traditional education, an educator is not usually specifically trained to deal with issues of the psyche, and a licensed mental health professional is generally not trained to provide an educational experience for clients. If the lines are blurred between mental health and education/learning, either professional may find themselves acting outside of their scope of practice.

Additionally, qualifications and licensure are not the only consideration when defining scope of practice. Your area of expertise is also important. By this, I am referring to your experience with a specific client population. For example, if you are working with veterans, do you have the knowledge, skills, and training to provide a safe and effective program for military personnel? Or if you are planning to offer a program to work with at-risk youth, do you have an understanding of the cultural and socio-economic challenges these young people face? It is imperative that you are able to navigate the nuances of each client group you serve in order to provide a safe and successful program.

As practitioners, we come across a diverse range of client populations, each with their own set of challenges and needs. As part of the process for both HERD models, we begin with conducting a thorough needs analysis or in-take assessment. Regardless of the client population served, this is an important part of the process of designing a program curriculum and/or treatment planning.

In the following chapters, you will see that within the HERD models, we emphasize that the ultimate aim of any session is to cultivate relationships—among clients/participants, horses, and the facilitators—so that clients/participants can experience something meaningful to take back into their everyday lives.

Why Does This Distinction Matter?

Why is it so important to distinguish between EFP and EFL? For those of you who are already offering such programs, you will know that there is a wide range of activities and groups that fall under the banner of EFL. Some of these involve very vulnerable populations, so it is important that we stay within our scope of practice so as not to cross over into a psychotherapy or counseling process where we may not have the skills to contain whatever is emerging. Nor do we want to open up any previous trauma for these individuals. As the field of equine-facilitated work grows, it becomes increasingly imperative that facilitators, regardless of scope of practice, engage in trauma-informed practice. Sarah Schlote, [3] founder of EQUUSOMA®, is an advocate for human–horse trauma recovery and believes that the work conducted within equine-facilitated sessions necessitates an understanding of what trauma is/is not, in order to ensure safe practice. This is particularly so if one is targeting client populations that will undoubtedly have experienced trauma of some kind—such as veterans, women from domestic abuse situations, at-risk youth, etc. In other words, knowing that there is a boundary is not sufficient for practitioners; the skill is in recognizing how to facilitate a session within the safe confines of that boundary and still work with participants in a deep and meaningful way.

The HERD Equine-Facilitated Psychotherapy (EFP) Model™

The HERD EFP Model consists of five stages:

- Sharing Space
- Release and Expand
- Deepening
- Coming Home to Relationships
- Integration

These stages were informed by the research I conducted for my doctoral program and reflect the philosophical and theoretical foundations of my psychotherapy training.

While the model does not always emerge within sessions as a linear process, these stages are recognizable in the therapeutic process as distinct stages of healing and growth. Beginning with the process of **Sharing Space,** clients may start their journey while being supported by their therapist to notice how they enter into relationships. This intentional act of bringing awareness to the relational space between self, other, and environment allows clients to slow down, become more centered, and breathe more deeply. This leads to the second stage of **Release and Expand**, where clients can begin to find some freedom from internalized constraints by challenging the limitations they place on themselves in order to broaden their horizons. Taking the risk towards authenticity leads to the third stage of **Deepening** connections and relationships with others, which in turn facilitates the process of **Coming Home to Relationships:** authentic relationships with self, other, and environment. It is this moment-to-moment unfolding of the fullness of one's bodily and emotional existence that culminates in the final stage of **Integration** of their experiences. This integration leads to an all-encompassing and enduring process through the whole of one's bodily being and is held with a sense of timelessness.

The HERD Equine-Facilitated Learning (EFL) Model™

In contrast, the HERD EFL Model consists of three stages:

- Meeting
- Relating
- Integrating

The differences in the two models reflect the distinct scope of practice considerations between EFP and EFL. The first stage, **Meeting**, focuses on the process of meeting our clients' needs, meeting our participants, and meeting the horses. The second stage, **Relating**, emphasizes the way we relate to our participants. It is based on a philosophical approach known as a phenomenological way of relating and offers a reflective and inclusive experience for participants. Stage three, **Integrating**, focuses on how to integrate the learning participants achieve within EFL sessions into everyday life.

In the following chapters, we will discuss the philosophical and theoretical foundations of both models, explore how these inform our practice through the use of case studies, and identify ways to create safe and ethical programs for your clients and participants. For a more detailed discussion of the HERD models and the different stages within them, please refer to my first book, *Equine-Facilitated Psychotherapy and Learning: The Human–Equine Relational Development (HERD) Approach.*

Chapter 4

Theory Foundations
of the HERD Models

Regardless of scope of practice, both of the HERD models are rooted in the same philosophical and theoretical foundations. There are currently many different approaches to working within an equine-facilitated setting, where trainers and practitioners, influenced by a diverse philosophical and theoretical base, offer their services to various client populations. Leif Hallberg[1] points out that there has been a lack of clarity to support the notion that equine-facilitated work can be deemed as a stand-alone educational or therapeutic method, with its own theories and constructs. Rather, practitioners have incorporated the theories from their educational, coaching, counseling, or psychotherapy modalities with their work with horses. This has led to a confusing mix of methodologies, where practitioners themselves may also find themselves at odds with their own values and beliefs about the way they practice.

In order to promote equine-facilitated psychotherapy and learning as an educational and therapeutic method in its own right, we need to address the philosophical foundations, examine the internal conflicts that arise when we are working against them, and look for the common ground between the different approaches to equine-facilitated work.

Why Philosophy?

What is the relevance of philosophy in equine-facilitated work? Philosophy is often seen as an obscure and exclusionary language, limited to the realms of the ivory towers of academia, and much too abstract for everyday life. It is a complex discipline that examines the mysteries of existence and reality and explores the relationships between humanity and nature, and self and environment. In this chapter, I want to shift your belief about philosophy and acknowledge it for what it is: the central foundations for all that we believe, cultivated from an attitude of awe and wonder for the world we live in. Philosophy challenges us to think deeply, more critically, and to live with integrity. It is, in fact, the perfect starting point for all our interactions with horses, so that we can stand clear in what we believe in as a modality.

As equine-facilitated practitioners, we are most concerned with how to bring what we know about horses and human relationships into a meaningful experience with our clients/participants, to support their learning and healing while adhering to our ethical principles. Philosophy examines *what* we know, and *how* we know what we know. It also challenges us to consider *how* we experience what we know and what we should do with what we know—that is, our ethics.

Many equine-facilitated practitioners have integrated philosophical language into their vocabulary, often through osmosis, without really questioning what it means. You might hear people referring to horses as authentic beings who mirror our emotions through being embodied in their relationships or talk about an I–Thou encounter with these majestic partners, with the assumption that we are all speaking from the same page. These are actually philosophical terms with specific meanings that have a direct impact on how we work with our clients and horses, so it is imperative that we understand them. In reality, there may be fundamental differences in our personal philosophies from which we approach the work. These differences may appear as outward inconsistencies and may reduce the validity of our modality in the eyes of our colleagues who work outside of the equine-facilitated domain. It is time to unpack these assumptions and examine how they fit with our underlying beliefs.

Philosophical Contradictions in Equine-Facilitated Work

Here are some examples of where the philosophy and the action, or behavior, of the practitioner may be misaligned:

Contradiction 1: The Horse is My Partner, But I Use My Horse as a Tool.

Remember when we discussed the importance of language? This inconsistency shows up in the way that we talk about our work and how we incorporate the horses. Committing to the use of the word "partnership" means we need to ensure that our language is consistent. In keeping with this partnership view, we need to make sure that the activities or exercises that we introduce as part of any equine-facilitated program are in line with our stated values of partnership. For example, there has been a trend lately of combining horses and yoga. While I understand the concept and theory behind how the horses' presence can provide an added element of Zen and mindfulness for participants, actually practicing yoga on the horse while someone holds the horse in place on a tight lead rope becomes somewhat problematic to align with our philosophy of partnership. This feels more like using the horse as a yoga mat and a tool rather than focusing on the relational partnership between horse and human. I'm not suggesting that horses and yoga can't be combined into a coherent philosophy and way of working, just that we need to be mindful of how we do that in practice.

Another inconsistency that often shows up is when we talk about partnering with our horses, but then do not take into account the context of how the horses are being introduced into the session. Imagine that we are offering an equine-facilitated learning session designed for working with survivors of sexual abuse. The aim of the session is to learn about boundaries, and the planned activity teaches the participants about grooming while the horses are standing in cross-ties.

While grooming might provide a number of teachable moments and benefits for the participants during the session, our philosophical stance of partnering with horses in this example needs to be examined. As the practitioner, how much attention do you pay to the fact that the horses are in cross-ties and, therefore, have no choice to move away from the interactions? If we do not acknowledge this aspect of the process, what are we teaching this particular client population about consent? If we do bring this into the process, what meaning might they make from the horse not having choice?

While many horses are happy to engage in this type of activity and enjoy grooming, if we are truly committed to the idea that we are partnering with sentient beings, what assumptions are we making about the horses in this session? What difference would it make to position the activity where the horse's consent and boundaries are respected?

Of course, maintaining safety is critical in any activity that we introduce into the session, and working within the parameters of what is practical at a facility is important. While I have the option at my facility to offer this activity while the horses are at liberty, I know that this isn't always the case. So how can we modify this to find some middle ground? What difference would it make if the horses were on lead and allowed some movement? I have witnessed some profound healing and learning in moments where the horse is allowed to move closer to a client/participant while being groomed, as well as when they have chosen to step away.

Contradiction 2: Healing and Learning Happens through Authentic Relationships with Horses, But the Interactions Are Used as Metaphors Only.

If we truly believe that healing and learning occur through the authentic relationships that can happen between horses and humans, then we need to attend to the actual relationship that is emerging between our participants and horses rather than positioning the experience as a metaphor only. If we are positioning equine-facilitated work as a way to support our clients and participants to gain insight into their relationships outside of the barn, we need to pay attention to the experience of *how* they are relating to the horses and what meaning *they* are making of that experience, without interpreting it for them.

Included in this is the belief that horses act as our "mirrors" and will act out our inner emotions. This is particularly troublesome, because if we truly believe that our horses are our partners, with equal standing in the process, then what does it mean if we reduce them to an inanimate object of a mirror? Instead, the HERD models hold the belief that as sentient beings in their own right, the horses are much more than mirrors. Rather than simply reflecting our emotions, the horses *respond* to us emotionally, energetically, and physically.

Contradiction 3: We Want You to Experience Connecting with Horses Yourself, But We Tell You What You've Experienced.

If we are promoting equine-facilitated work as a way for participants to learn about how they interact in relationships, then we must work in a way that allows the clients/participants to make meaning of what they have experienced themselves, without interpretations by the facilitator. To go back to our grooming example, if we ask a client/participant to groom a horse and the horse stamps its foot, that interaction may be significant for that individual.

While we may have noticed the flies hovering around them, by stating that as the reason for the horse stamping, we are in danger of removing a meaningful experience for the client/participant. What is their experience in that moment of their relationship with the horse? Did they notice the stamping? Did they experience it as a relational rupture or an indication of impatience? How did they respond to that in the moment? Did they withdraw or persist? How might that impact the relationship between them? How might we facilitate connection after a rupture? There are so many possibilities that might emerge if we can hold off interpreting or offering a reason.

Key Principles of the HERD Philosophy

The HERD models are based on the following three key principles:

- Here & Now
- What & How
- I & Thou

Here & Now refers to the importance of being in the present moment. What & How, refers to the philosophical approach of phenomenology—a descriptive rather than interpretive way of working—and I & Thou refers to the philosophical concept of authenticity and connection based on the work of Martin Buber.[2]

Key Principle 1: Here & Now
The principle of Here-and-now refers to our ability to remain in the present moment in a fully embodied way. This includes not only our awareness of what we are thinking, but also what we are feeling in our body through all of our senses. It also incorporates what our intuitive feelings in each moment might be.

Ultimately, all experience occurs in the present moment, and there is only this moment right now. The past has gone and the future is yet to be, so in recognizing the importance of the present moment, we can let go of everything else. This allows us to be fully available for connection with another being. Paying attention to the Here-and-Now has become more mainstream in the Western world in the past couple of decades, and yet it comes from centuries-old traditions in the East. Thích Nhất Hạnh, a Buddhist monk and mindfulness teacher, says that we need to "Live the actual moment. Only this actual moment is life."

This mantra serves us well when we are entering into an equine-facilitated session. As practitioners, it is vital that we engage with our clients/participants from a grounded place and be fully aware of what is happening around us in each given moment. Of course, it's easier said than done, and for many of us it is a practice that needs continuous cultivation.

Levels of Here & Now Awareness. Within existential–humanistic psychology and Gestalt psychotherapy, the here and now is a fundamental practice. I say practice because that's what it takes. To focus our attention on the present moment, in each moment, is not an easy task. Life is complicated, chaotic, and in constant motion. It pulls us into a whirlwind of what, ifs, and if onlys, shuttling our attention away from the here and now and to the there and then; we worry about what has passed and fret about what is yet to come. This is part of the human condition, and while there is nothing wrong with that process, it can create stress and anxiety for us. That's not to say that there is no value in allowing our minds to wander to the future; after all, it is often through daydreaming about what might be that we can allow our dreams to come to fruition. However, if you find that you are living more in the there and then rather than the here and now, what might you be missing out on in this moment?

When we are in the here and now, we can feel our own presence, both bodily and energetically. Of course, it's not a case of all or nothing. We are often fleeting in our ability to stay present and aware of the shuttling back and forth and/or half-in/half-out moments. In an effort to practice the art of staying present, it is useful to be able to differentiate between different levels of awareness. This is something that we can teach our participants too. This is not about meditation, but an active noticing of what is happening in each moment. I like to think of this as three levels of awareness: Self, Other, and Environment.

Awareness of Self in the here and now begins with the internal sensations, emotions, and movements that you notice moment by moment. For example, if you were to close your eyes right now, what do you become aware of in yourself? How is your breathing? Fast or slow? Deep or shallow? What about the muscle tension in your face, jaw, neck, and shoulders? How might you release that tension through your breath? What emotions are you beginning to experience as you pay attention to these sensations, and what movements might you want to make? Are you able to do all that without judgment of yourself? Are you able to hold a sense of compassion for your own process? Notice that the focus is more on the *experience* of the moment rather than your thoughts about it.

Awareness of Other in the here and now begins with noticing how the other is relating to you (or not). What do you notice about their proximity or distance? Is their energy faster or slower than yours? How might you get in tune with them? What do you experience?

Awareness of Environment: What else is present in the environment? What is on the horizon of your awareness? Can you zoom in and out between the detail and the bigger picture? Can you soften your eyes to take in the periphery?

In practicing our ability to notice our flow of attention between self, other, and environment in each moment, we can become more fluid as a facilitator in sessions with participants.

Benefits of Here & Now Awareness. There are numerous physiological benefits of being in the here and now.

- When we focus our attention on the present moment, we are able to breathe more deeply. This, in turn, decreases our heart rate and lowers our blood pressure.
- It improves our circulation, which increases blood flow to vital organs and increases our energy levels.
- It improves mental acuity—our concentration and focus improve and we can think more clearly.
- It decreases the production of the stress hormone cortisol. Cortisol production puts a strain on our adrenal glands. Chronic stress and adrenal fatigue can often cause immune system imbalances. Decreasing stress levels allows our immune system to re-balance.

Psychologically, being in the here and now benefits us by:

- Allowing us to accept what is, and thereby freeing ourselves from the shoulda/woulda/coulda moments in our lives. Eckhart Tolle,[3] author of *The Power of Now*, says that the moment that judgment stops by accepting what is, we can be free of our mind.

- By staying in the here and now, we are also more able to access our emotional responses without being clouded by judgments. In Gestalt therapy terms, we refer to this as our response-ability, or our ability to respond to any given situation in a more intentional rather than reactive way.

All of this leads to our ability to become more connected in our relationships. As we've discussed, in doing this work, it is all about relationships: how we relate and interact with each other from a place of compassion, integrity, and, above all, awareness of self, other, and environment. This can only happen if we are grounded in the here and now. As practitioners, this means being able to hold the space in a safe and compassionate way to allow for learning to emerge. Eckhart Tolle emphasized that the power of now can only be realized in the moment, and that putting effort into it already takes us away from the present moment, as it implies that we are trying to get to somewhere else. By welcoming the moment as it is, we can allow ourselves to stay present.

How does this relate to horses? Horses are herd animals and are always aware of the present moment. It's not only their survival instinct but also their way of being. Horses rely on energetic presence. Yes, they need to be aware of where there is a potential threat, but it is also their way of interacting with one another in the herd. The past is the past, and the future is not a concern. All that matters is the here and now.

In bringing clients/participants to the herd, by practicing the art of staying in the here and now, we can relate this to what is happening in the session. Within an equine-facilitated session, through guiding attention from self, other, and environment, we can facilitate an increased awareness of the present-moment experience. People may begin to notice how this relates to the horses' way of being or start to see how their interactions impact others in the group. This heightened awareness both intra-personally (i.e., their internal process) and interpersonally (i.e. their external process) may emerge through their interactions with the horses and with one another, and/or you.

This is particularly effective when working with individuals on the autism spectrum and with at-risk youth and military personnel who may be struggling with their social interactions or relationships in general. Above all, it is about heart-centered connection.

Key Principle 2: What & How
What and How refers to the process by which the equine-facilitated practitioner holds a sense of curiosity about what is unfolding in the relationship between the client/participant and the horses, without jumping to our own interpretations but simply reflecting back our observations to them and allowing them to make meaning of this themselves.

This process is based on the **philosophical concept of phenomenology.** This approach focuses on the individual's worldview—their perspective of the world and their experiences. It is through the use of description rather than interpretation that meaning is made from each experience.

Phenomenology is a branch of philosophy related to the study *of* experience and *how* we experience. This concept was developed by a German philosopher, Edmund Husserl, who focused on the idea that all experience is subjective—i.e., from an individual's own perspective. Taken from the Greek word *phainomenon*, meaning "appearances," phenomenology can be understood as the *study of the perception of experience.* This idea gained ground through the work of French philosopher Maurice Merleau-Ponty.[4] He argued that experiences are not simply thoughts but a whole-body phenomenon. This includes both passive experiences such as sensations as well as more active processes such as imagination, behaviors, emotions, and intentions. In this way, phenomenology is an individual's process *as it is lived through and experienced in embodied awareness.*

I'd like to point out here that this is a very brief introduction to phenomenology. There are scholars who have spent their entire careers examining the nuances of this branch of philosophy, and we are merely scratching the surface of the tip of this iceberg. Specifically, we are referring to the branch of phenomenology known as existential phenomenology. Essentially, we are asking, "What is the lived experience of this person, and what does it mean to them?"

With that in mind, can you see how that links to our first key principle of Here & Now? What we're looking at essentially is what is happening for our clients/participants, how they are experiencing what is happening, and the meaning they make from it in that moment.

Relating to Clients/Participants. So now that we have the philosophical concept in place, how does that actually work in practice? In order to work in a phenomenological way, and for our clients/participants to make meaning for themselves of what is happening for them, we need to let go of our preconceived ideas, opinions, and what we think they might be experiencing. Instead, we describe what we see happening in the interactions between them and the horses and allow them to draw their own conclusions. This is easier said than done, of course! *Say what you see, not what you think* needs to be a mantra for us all as facilitators, and it takes practice.

This is a challenge to many people who have been around horses for a long time. We are so used to reading and interpreting their signals to us that it has almost become unconscious and second nature. I also don't know a single person who is familiar and fond of animals who doesn't engage in some level of anthropomorphism in their interactions with animals—that is, ascribing human qualities, emotions, and behaviors to the animals.

Now, if we were to delve further into the philosophy of this, we could get ourselves tangled up in another debate about whether there is a difference between animal emotions and human emotions, since, of course, humans are also animals. Let's save that conversation for another time. But I would like to refer you to the authors Carl Safina[5] and Peter Wohlleben[6] for some fascinating reading on that subject. Safina is the author of *Beyond Words: What animals Think and Feel,* and Wohlleben has written a series of books about the inner lives of animals. All of it is fascinating stuff that highlights the human-centric assumptions that we have made in the way that we relate to the natural world around us, and the beings that we share this planet with.

Back to my original point... In order to relate to our clients/participants from a phenomenological approach, it is necessary to put aside what you think you know about horses, and trust that your clients/participants will make sense of the interactions themselves without placing your perspective into the mix. Let me say that again. It's necessary to put aside what you think you know about horses, and trust that they will make sense of the interactions themselves. This doesn't mean that you ignore signs from the horses with regard to safety or welfare, but when it comes to an interaction that could be a healing or learning point for your client/participant, to step away from your own interpretation of what is happening and allow them to make sense of it.

Of course, this depends on the type of equine-facilitated session you are running. If you are conducting an EFL session that is geared towards learning about horse behavior as a way for participants to translate that to their own ways of interacting with people, then some teaching about horse behavior will be required. Working in a phenomenological way doesn't mean that you cannot include some teaching about horse behavior, and/or horse communication signals, etc. I am referring specifically to those moments in a session when the clients/participants are interacting with the horses as part of an activity that is designed to elicit personal insight.

What do you see? Let's give this a go...

What do you see in this picture? Take a few moments to write down a description.

Did you use any of the following words, or variations of these words? Happy, connected, interested, engaged, curious...in other words, any adjectives that convey emotion? If so, that's not what you see; it's the meaning that you've made from what you see. If you said, "I see the participant looking at the horse and standing with her hands holding a hula-hoop, with her left leg crossed in front of her right. I see the horse has her hind left leg stretched out behind her, with her head in line with the participant, outside the hula-hoop" then that's a *description* of the picture.

See the difference?

The story behind this photo is a good example of the importance of working phenomenologically. This was taken during an EFL training event at The HERD Institute. This student had stepped up and volunteered to be a participant as part of the demo, and had chosen to work with my mare, Cheyenne. During the session, the participant was talking about how she struggled to make space for herself in her busy life. As a new mom, it was hard for her to focus on herself, hold her boundaries but still maintain space for some fun. We began to experiment with the hula-hoop as a representation of how she might bring more "fun" into her life. As she spoke about this, Cheyenne began to walk towards her, and the participant chose to move to avoid getting in Cheyenne's way. Then, Cheyenne changed directions and headed straight for the participant again. She stopped next to the participant, yawned, and stretched out her hind leg (when this picture was taken), and then moved her head into the hula-hoop, bringing her head closer to the participant's chest. And there she stayed.

The group that was observing the demo all giggled. Turning to the participant, I described what I was seeing and asked her what she made of it all. To the group's surprise, she responded by saying that she felt intruded upon. In holding onto the hula-hoop, she had experienced a clearer sense of needing to hold her boundaries and was enjoying walking around the arena (which was fun). So when Cheyenne headed in her direction, she wanted to hold her boundaries while having fun, and was fine until Cheyenne stuck her head inside the hula-hoop. As she said this, Cheyenne backed up out of the hula-hoop, and continued to stand next to the participant. The participant laughed and took Cheyenne's moving to be an acknowledgment of her need to hold her boundaries.

In debriefing after the session, a few of the group members expressed their surprise at the participant's interpretation of what had happened. They felt joy in the moment when Cheyenne had placed her head inside the hula-hoop, thinking that this was Cheyenne's invitation to play and have fun. Instead, by working phenomenologically, and not allowing our own interpretations to color the feedback to the participant, she was able to make meaning of the interaction herself and came up with something relevant for her.

How do you provide that feedback? How might you describe what's happening in the picture above? How would you provide that feedback to your client/participant? By focusing on the description rather than the interpretation, we can hold space for them to lean into the experience and learn from it. So in the picture, an interpretation might be: "I see how playful Cheyenne is being with you" or, "I think she wants to play with the hula-hoop. Feedback in this instance might be: "I see Cheyenne standing still with her hind leg stretched out."

In providing the feedback, focus on what is happening by *describing* what you see, not what *you* think the horse is saying. Psychologically, "a-ha moments," of sudden realization, inspiration, or insight tend to occur when we connect the dots ourselves, and not from others telling us what something is, or should be, or what it means. These a-ha moments are much easier to hold on to if they emerged from within. So, allowing our clients/participants to create that link for themselves is really important, and the way we do that is to hold the space, breathe, and trust that process.

What is happening right now? One way to be able to continuously re-focus on the here and now in a phenomenological way is to ask the question "What is happening right now?" This can be followed by "How is that impacting your relationship with...?" Other examples of ways to elicit experienced-based and meaningful responses might be:

- I notice that when you _____, (groom/stroke/lead), the horse responds by _____ (turning her head/moving away/standing really still). What do you make of that?
- What is happening between you all right now?
- How are you communicating with each other right now?
- What do you notice in your breathing right now?
- Who else does this resonate with?
- How might this experience change how you relate to others in your life?

Notice that these questions are all based on increasing awareness of the relational process in each moment, and not on what or who the horse reminds the client/participant of. In this way, we are working on the actual, developing, and authentic relationship with the horses rather than only focusing on metaphors. While metaphors can be useful as a vehicle towards awareness of the lived experience in the relationship, it may form a barrier to the potential authentic connection. In reality, there are a hundred different questions you could ask as a follow up to the description that you give, and the meaning that your clients/participants make of the situation. Always return your attention to what is happening in the relationship and the awareness between self, other, and environment.

A Note on Scope of Practice. While the phenomenological description in the feedback that we provide is the same whether we are working in an EFL or EFP context, we need to be mindful that the follow-up questions that we ask do not step outside of our scope of practice. For EFL practitioners, focusing on questions that evoke deep feelings may land us in hot water and increases the potential of touching on traumatic experiences that fall outside our scope. For mental health practitioners who are also providing EFL sessions, it is here that the biggest challenge arises. Just because we are licensed to provide therapy and have the training to do so does not mean that we have the consent from our EFL participants to go there.

Sarah Schlote[7] of EQUUSOMA® talks about trauma in the form of a sandwich. The bread or bun on the top and bottom of the sandwich represents how we orient ourselves to the world around us. The lettuce, tomato, and whatever other garnishes represent the resources in our lives that help to support us in our experiencing. The burger, deli-meat, or whatever is at the core of the sandwich represents any trauma that we may have experienced in our lives.

I find that this is a useful way to distinguish between EFL and EFP in terms of scope of practice, and in thinking about the types of questions we can ask our clients/participants. Within an EFL context, I might ask questions to ascertain details about the bread and garnishes. I might get really curious about the taste and the texture of these elements of the sandwich and explore what options there might be to change these elements if desired. I might also want to know what type of filling the sandwich has—ham, cheese, turkey, peanut butter—but it would be outside of my scope of practice to elicit answers about further details of this, such as how many slices of ham or cheese, or whether it's crunchy or smooth peanut butter, and especially what it tastes like or how it feels to eat the sandwich.

So, in an EFL setting, I might be working with a client population of adolescents who have experienced sexual abuse, and my program might offer learning experiences to increase self-confidence and awareness of boundaries. The sandwich filling in this instance is sexual abuse. I know it's there, but I'm not going to ask questions that might open up descriptions of that experience from my participants. Instead, we stick with questions that help them orient themselves to the self, other, and environment and highlight what resources (garnishes) they might have or need in order to support an increase in self-confidence.

Reflective and Inclusive. In focusing on the interactions between clients/participants, as well as their own inner shifts in awareness between self, other, and environment, we can create a space for a reflective process. Whatever is emerging in each moment is set against the background of the participants' lives. Whether you are working with an organizational team, or individuals who have never met prior to this session, or in a one-to-one context, each client/participant brings with them their own perspective and lived experiences that impact on their way of relating to others. It is through this phenomenological way of working that we can hold the intention to be inclusive of all of their background while attending to what is significant for them in each moment. In this way, we can get closer to meeting our clients and participants where they are, not where we want them to be.

Key Principle 3: I &Thou

For me, the most wonderful thing about working in an equine-facilitated environment is to know that the philosophy behind what we are doing stems from horses themselves.

Martin Buber[8] was a Jewish philosopher who spent a lot of time at his grandfather's ranch as he was growing up. His experiences with horses, and his observations of their interactions, prompted the young philosopher to ask some fundamental questions about how we bring ourselves into relationships. His philosophy is one that is deeply relational in approach and focuses on the intersubjectivity (i.e., the bi-directional experiencing) of those within the relationship. In other words, what happens in "the between" of the experience is made up of the subjective experience of both parties.

As Buber was grooming his horse one day, he noticed the difference in how the quality of the interaction changed depending on how present he was with the horse. He described this process as one of being *fully with* the horse versus experiencing the moment objectively. He noticed that when he was simply grooming his horse and enjoying the experience, he was completely immersed in the moment between himself and this other being. He was aware of how his horse was responding to him in his ability to be with him. As his mind drifted away, and the grooming experience became more task focused (i.e., the need to get him clean), the quality of contact and relationship changed to a more functional one. He felt himself pulling away from the experience and the relationship and noticed that his horse responded differently too.

This was the experience from which his philosophy of I–Thou emerged. Buber described the difference between an I–Thou way of relating versus an I–It approach. The I–Thou acknowledges the moment of connection between self and other, and I–It refers to a more objectified stance.

Buber's I–Thou. In life, there are moments of connection between self and other that are deeply moving and impactful. These are precious moments when that connection is felt at a deep level within ourselves, when we feel that we are truly seen; and yet that moment not only impacts us but also the other. This way of relating speaks to those moments when we are truly with another, knowing that the experience changes both parties. These moments cannot be forced but emerge through staying open hearted and willing, and taking the risk that the other can see us fully. Buber says, "The *Thou* meets me through grace – it is not found by seeking...but I step into direct relation with it. Hence the relation means being chosen and choosing...I become through my relation to the *Thou;* as I become *I,* I say *Thou.*"

This is one of my favorite quotes. There's so much beauty within it that even reading this gives me goose bumps. The idea is that connection and relationship constitute an intersubjective experience: It happens between two beings, whether it be horse or human, and *both* are changed by it. This isn't the same as the idea that we become whole through being with another—more that when we are seen fully by another, as we see the other fully, we can expand into more of who we are. Cue theme song from *The Greatest Showman.*

Buber Says that All Real Living is Meeting. What he means is that it is in those moments of connection that we are truly alive. His reference to "real living" speaks to our ability to be authentic in those moments of connection, that there is no real connection if we cannot be authentic or allow ourselves to see the other's authenticity. Gestalt therapist Ruella Frank [9] refers to these moments as "I see you see me, I feel you feel me."

Me, Thee, We. Brené Brown[10], social researcher and author of *Daring Greatly*, speaks about the need for vulnerability in order to connect authentically. She says that vulnerability is a prerequisite for intimacy and that connection is what gives purpose and meaning to our lives. For Martin Buber, these intimate, I–Thou moments can only occur when both parties allow themselves to be vulnerable in some way.

So, can we be open hearted and give ourselves to the relationship in a way that leaves us vulnerable? Gestalt therapists Erv and Miriam Polster [11] talk about the risk that is required in truly meeting another. In another one of my favorite quotes of all time, they say that,

> It's not just togetherness or joining. It can only happen between separate beings, always requiring independence and always risking capture in the union. At the moment of union, one's fullest sense of his person is swept along into a new creation. I am no longer only me, but me and thee make we.

This is the essence of the I–Thou way of relating. Are you willing to take that risk, to be brave and trust another? Are you prepared to be changed by this moment of connection? Will you allow me to journey with you so that we can experience something together that is unique to us?

Relating to Clients and Participants. How do we translate this philosophical concept into working with our participants? There are three elements to consider:

- I–Thou and Presence
- I–Thou and Awareness
- I–It is Needed

I–Thou and Presence. Here, we are referring to your presence, the horse's presence, and the client/participant's presence. Existential psychologist James Bugental[12] said that presence is

> the skill of being able to simultaneously be open and available to the experience of your clients and yourself, and responding from the immediacy of that experience. It is your ability to stay with the process that is unfolding in the moment, while holding space for all possibilities.

Tracking where we are in each moment, and grounding ourselves in the here and now, will allow us to be fully present to what is unfolding in the session between our clients/participants and horses, as well as with us. The most precious gift we can offer others is our presence—that is, our undivided attention in the moment. As we listen and observe our participants, we allow the phenomenological process to unfold and support our clients/participants to make meaning of the experience themselves. Remember, we want to hear the story first and let the meaning unfold, rather than to be present with expectations of a certain significance into which all behavior is then fitted.

As discussed previously, the reason that horses are such good partners in this work is that their very existence requires them to be present, in the here and now, at all times. When they show up, they really show up! Additionally, the horses not only embody an energetic quality with their presence, but they help us to get embodied in ourselves.

Tracking our clients/participants' ability to stay present is a challenge. This is why it's helpful sometimes to begin with breathing and grounding exercises, so that they can return to these techniques throughout the session (with or without us prompting). Of course, if you are not present in the moment yourself, then it makes it much harder to get a sense of where they are. The skill needed to support another's ability to remain present-centered comes from practicing being in the moment ourselves. There's an energetic quality that comes from being in the moment that is felt on an embodied level.

I–Thou and Awareness. Remember the concept of the different levels of awareness of self, other, and environment? We'll start joining the dots here. Awareness can be viewed as how someone experiences and interprets the here and now. It's their understanding of what they are doing, and how they are doing it (see how this fits with phenomenology of the what and how?). Awareness is also the knowledge that we are responsible for our actions and our choices (response-ability). So, basically, it is the deliberate and conscious act of paying attention to all our physical sensations, thoughts, and feelings about what is happening to me in the environment I'm in, in each moment. So, awareness is an embodied process.

Simple, right?

So how does this connect with Buber's I–Thou? Buber talks about what is created in the space between self and other in an I–Thou moment. Bringing our awareness to the inbetween space allows us to highlight those moments of connection and disconnection between self, other, and environment.

This means that when we are working with our horses and clients/participants, we are also able to notice and increase our awareness of these shifts between them and the horses, as well as with ourselves.

I–It is Needed. Buber says that when we are operating from an I–It stance there is a disconnect in the relationship. If the *I–Thou* refers to a meeting in which one approaches the other as another being (a "who"), then *I–It* refers to the turning of the other into an object or "thing.. It's the difference between being present with some*one* and talking to them about some*thing*. It's the difference between feeling heard in a conversation, and someone talking *at* you. It's the difference between being with the horses in partnership and treating them as a tool in the work we do.

Buber's philosophical language gets lost in translation sometimes, and people grasp onto the idea that an I–Thou way of relating is the "right" way. There's a misunderstanding that you must stay in I–Thou connection at all times. This is not what Buber intended and, more important, it is simply impossible. In reality, the opportunities to connect with self, other, and environment are abundant, but we naturally drift in and out of the two states of I–Thou and I–It continuously. This is not only natural, but necessary. That's why we call it an I–Thou *moment*. They are fleeting, precious, and deeply felt, but the minute we try to hold on to the moment, we have already moved away from the experience and turned that into an I–It.

For many of us, when first introduced to these philosophical concepts, it all feels pretty mind-bending and confusing. In the attempt to wrap our heads around it, we may feel frustrated at the archaic language and perhaps question the point of philosophical discussions at all. It's hard to see how these highly academic principles might apply in real life. I get it. Really, I do! I also know that by wrapping our heads around these concepts, we can transform our relationships not only with our clients/participants and horses but also in our everyday lives by being more mindful of how we step in and out of connection and live more authentically.

I truly believe that if we are to offer our clients/participants something real and meaningful, then we need to examine our understanding of what "real and meaningful" is. Within this industry, we talk about the horses always bringing themselves authentically into each moment, and that they are always congruent in themselves. But what does that actually mean? And how is that related to Buber?

Authenticity. Existential psychologist James Bugental says that the road towards authenticity is paved with present-centered awareness. It is a central genuineness and awareness of being where an authentic individual possesses three main characteristics:

- an awareness of themselves, their relationships, and the context within which they live
- an acceptance that living is a process of making choices
- an understanding that all choices and decisions require the acceptance of responsibility and consequences.

You see how all the philosophical threads are beginning to come together now? The first point here is what we've been talking about in terms of awareness of self, other, and environment. The second point is that to live authentically is a choice—what we do and how we do it—tying in with our phenomenological worldview. Third is that all choices and decisions require acceptance of responsibility and consequences; this is the idea of response-ability, or our ability to respond to what is happening in each moment. Weaving throughout these elements is the constant flow of the I–Thou and I–It way of relating to the world. And in stepping into each I–Thou encounter, I am bringing myself into it with authenticity, taking the risk to be vulnerable with the other and be changed by the experience.

Inter-species I–Thou. To step into an I–Thou relation with a non-human animal is to acknowledge that humans are not the measure of all things. With the growing evidence on the therapeutic benefits of human–animal bonds and the physiological impact of being with horses, it is possible to view the connections made between clients/participants and horses through an I–Thou lens. As with human-to-human relationships, there is a continuous flow between the I–Thou and I–It, during an equine-facilitated session. The HERD approach focuses on increasing awareness of these shifts in each moment as a way to enable clients/participants to embody their ability to connect and disconnect in their relationships.

The HERD approach promotes the theory that first there is awareness, and then there is choice. The practitioner draws the clients'/participants' attention to what is happening in the moment, both internally (sensations and emotions) and relationally (with others), focusing on the quality of connection between the clients/participants and their environment. In this way, we can focus our attention on *what* is happening for them and *how* it impacts them.

Applying this philosophy within the context of equine-facilitated work requires that the practitioner meet the clients/participants as a fellow traveler on a shared journey. Rather than stepping into performing a "role," this model requires us to bring ourselves authentically into the encounter on an embodied level.

I–Thou in Everyday Life. I–Thou moments have the potential to appear in relationships at any given time—if we stay open and available for connection. I–Thou moments may appear in everyday life at the most unexpected times and may fundamentally change who we are and what we believe about ourselves, or they can be simple, quiet exchanges that shift our experience of ourselves.

So far, we've talked about I–Thou moments as deep moments of connection between two beings. The mutual connection, the way it changes and shapes both parties, and the meaningful nature of that moment all make it appear as though this is serious stuff, right?

The answer is that we don't truly know unless we are part of that connection. I–Thou moments may be deep, quiet, and reflective moments of connection: lovers staring into each other's eyes or a soft nicker as your horse approaches you. It can be the acknowledgment of trust when someone hands over their baby to you for the first time, or the uncontrollable laughter of a shared joke between friends, or the focused determination of a shared endeavor. Connection, authenticity, and transformation happen in all kinds of ways, and look and feel different every time.

This might seem obvious now that we've pointed it out, but in truth, so often I find myself forgetting that lightheartedness as a shared moment can be equally life changing for someone as a moment of deep, shared contemplation.

When we put this into the context of how this emerges within an equine-facilitated setting, and what this means with how we work from a phenomenological perspective, the fact that we cannot assume what an I–Thou moment looks like for another becomes crucial. Remember, Buber says, "The thou meets me through grace...It cannot be found through seeking."

It's All about Relationships! In our quest to honor our intentions of adhering to our philosophical beliefs, there is often a paradoxical disconnect between philosophical foundations, theory, and practice. It is important to understand that within the philosophical traditions of embodied phenomenology and Buber's I–Thou, practitioners do not translate this process to idealize an embodied, authentic, I–Thou connection. What I mean by this is that it would be easy for students of this approach to turn the I–Thou connection into an aim for our clients/participants. Paradoxically, not only does this remove the possibility for such a connection as the process becomes one of achieving an agenda rather than honoring the relational process, but in fact becomes a distortion of Buber's philosophy, which emphasizes the importance of the movement between the I–Thou and I–It ways of relating, and acknowledges the impermanence of the I–Thou moment. In the attempt to hold on to that moment, we have already moved into an I–It.

The HERD approach brings into focus the movement between these moments, paying attention to the embodied nature of the encounters for both the clients/participants and the horses. By honoring the philosophical framework that supports this process, we can translate this into theoretical concepts that reflect our beliefs and, in turn, apply them in practice. Ultimately, we return to our fundamental belief that it's all about relationships.

I am fully aware that this I–Thou concept may be difficult to grasp, particularly as so much of it can only be solidified through experiencing that moment. So, I want to share a personal example with you to enable you to relate to this from a heartfelt place rather than a cognitive space.

To Be Seen Fully

The Uber driver pulled up outside the gate to our farm, where I asked him to drop me off. It was 7.30 am, and I was returning home after getting the red-eye back to Florida from California. I had just spent the past ten days sitting with my beloved grandma in hospital, culminating in being by her side and holding her hand as she took her last breath just the day before. I was red-eyed from tears and exhaustion, and desperately needed to come home to be with my husband and animals. As I unlatched the gate, I saw my herd of three horses in their paddock at the end of our long driveway. It was breakfast time, and my friend Sarah had just arrived to feed them.

All three heads turned in my direction at the sound of the gate. I closed the gate behind me to begin the long walk down the driveway and sighed. I turned back towards the herd and saw that Arrow and Cheyenne had resumed their interest in Sarah and the sound of breakfast being dished out. Reba held my gaze.

I'm not sure which came first, the tears or the sound of her galloping towards me. I gravitated towards the fence, and Reba stretched her neck out over it and put her head on my chest. I reached up and put my arms around her neck and sobbed. She stood there while I cried for a few moments before taking a step back. We were eye to eye, and that moment allowed me to take a breath and center myself once more. In that moment, I felt fully seen as I experienced her fully: the maternal mare who recognized my grief and held space for me with compassion, and the nervous one in the herd who also needed to know that I was resilient enough to withstand this loss. As I exhaled, I stroked my beautiful girl on her shoulder, expressed my gratitude, and assured her that I would be fine. Slowly, we walked together as I made my way down the driveway, and she meandered back to the herd and her breakfast.

This I–Thou moment with Reba has sustained me through my ongoing grief from the loss of my grandma. The meaning that I made from that interaction has further strengthened my belief that our horses feel and respond to us in profound ways that we are yet to fully understand. My grief in that moment was raw and breathtaking, and I am grateful that I was able to allow myself to just be in the moment. In doing that, I felt fully seen by Reba, while simultaneously able to see her fully. I felt her support then and each time I remember that moment. The profound nature of these I–Thou moments become embedded into our bodily beings and offer the potential for change and healing.

Chapter 5

Diversity Considerations

Within any equine-facilitated setting, there will be times when a phenomenological way of working may not appear to be effective. Certainly, there may be times when asking questions or describing verbally what is going on may not be relevant. So far, we have looked at the practice of phenomenology within an equine-facilitated setting as "Say what you see." Of course, we need to acknowledge that for the most part, this is a neurotypical application of the concept. What if we are working with those who are neurodivergent? Our mantra for practitioners to "Say what you see" might appear out of alignment with our intention to be inclusive.

First, we need to have a clearer understanding of neurodiversity, what we mean by that, and how we can provide an inclusive environment. Those of you who work with vulnerable populations may be more familiar with this term than others; however, it is a concept that is important for all of us as practitioners to understand.

What is Neurodiversity?

Neurodiversity is the diversity of human brains and minds. It refers to the infinite variations in neurocognitive functioning within our species. To be truly inclusive in our practice, it is necessary for us to make the invisible visible. Working inclusively means that we need to become champions of the neurodiversity movement, a social justice movement that calls for a paradigm shift towards seeking civil rights, equality, respect, and full societal inclusion for the neurodivergent population. This means embracing the idea that neurodiversity is a natural and valuable form of human diversity, and that the idea that there is one "normal" or "healthy" type of brain or mind, or one "right" style of neurocognitive functioning is a culturally constructed fiction—no more valid (and no more conducive to a healthy society or to the overall well-being of humanity) than the idea that there is one "normal" or "right" ethnicity, gender, or culture.

The term neurodivergent is used to refer to individuals whose cognitive functioning falls outside of the dominant societal norms. Deborah Reber,[1] author of *Differently Wired: Raising an Exceptional Child in a Conventional World,* prefers the term "differently wired" to refer to individuals whose brain functions differently than those of "neurotypical" people. These differences in cognitive functioning may be diagnosed as autism, dyslexia, dyspraxia, or attention-deficit/hyperactivity disorder, or as a result of brain injury, drug addiction, or meditation practices. This is not an exhaustive list of the types of neurodivergent functioning that exist.

In contrast, those individuals who fall within the parameters of societal expectations of neurological functioning are deemed to be neurotypical. As with any majority/minority dynamic, the social dynamics that manifest in regard to neurodiversity are similar to those of other forms of human diversity, where neurodivergent individuals may often experience prejudice, misunderstanding, and/or oppression from the majority, neurotypical society. Steve Silberman,[2] author of *Neurotribes: The Legacy of Autism and the Future of Neurodiversity*, says that neurodiversity "should be regarded as naturally occurring cognitive variations with distinctive strengths that have contributed to the evolution of technology and culture rather than mere checklists of deficits and dysfunctions." So rather than working toward eliminating these differences, we need to embrace them.

How to Work Inclusively

What if your clients/participants are blind or hard of hearing? What if they are non-verbal and/or have cognitive challenges? What if you are working with little ones who don't yet have the language to respond or the capacity for self-awareness or reflection? What if you are working with an elderly population living with dementia or Alzheimer's, who are struggling to locate themselves in the moment? Does this mean that we cannot work from a phenomenological perspective? In practice, the HERD philosophy of focusing on the here and now, what and how, and I and Thou is relevant across all client populations. While there may be additional factors to take into consideration, and ways in which we can offer a truly inclusive approach specific to that population, the practice of the phenomenological description still holds.

Here's why: In all of the examples above, to not say what we see because of any of those factors means that we are making assumptions based on *what we think our clients/participants have the potential for.* To assume that someone with dementia is not able to understand or engage with you or that a non-verbal child does not have the cognitive ability to process what you are saying is to do them a disservice. While we can include other ways to aid their understanding and enhance their experience based on their specific needs, moving away from the phenomenological description naturally already, presupposes and frames the meaning that they might make from their experience.

For example, if you are working with an autistic* child who is non-verbal and you decide that because they are non-verbal to shift away from a phenomenological description, it does not give them the opportunity to tell you in their own way what meaning they are making of the experience. The major difference in this example is that while a neurotypical participant might be able to articulate their experience so you are clear about what meaning they've made, with a non-verbal participant we may not understand fully what they are communicating. This is a subtle but important shift. Rather than positioning the participant as being unable to do something, we are acknowledging their different way of operating and *our inability* to understand them. They are simply speaking a different language that we have yet to learn. This is also true for any of the other examples above.

I remember working with a group of middle school kids in a psycho-educational equine-facilitated session. These were all students with cognitive and/or physical challenges, a couple of whom were very limited in their speech and one who was non-verbal. In teaching the participants about personal hygiene and health, we had designed an activity to teach them to groom the horses. Drawing parallels with how they might keep themselves "well-groomed," we asked the participants to take turns grooming.

---

* I use the term autistic child not as a move away from person-first language, but as a way of acknowledging that autism is not something that the child is living with but something that is part of who the child is. We would not, for example, say that someone is living with blindness.

One participant was a twelve-year old boy with limited speech and cognitive challenges. Nick was a happy child, always smiling, with a cracking sense of humor. He liked to wink at all the women—teachers, aides, facilitators, and volunteers—and his zest for life was contagious. In this session, he had been brushing the horse's mane. I approached him as he was doing this and said, "I see you're brushing her mane slowly. What do you think that's like for her?" Nick looked up and smiled. Giggling, he brought his hand up to his shoulder and flicked his hand backwards away from himself and tossed his head sideways.

At first, I thought he was flicking dirt away from himself, but I was unsure whether this was it. So I asked him to do that action again. Tess, in that moment, shook her head, and her mane flicked past our faces. Nick laughed and pointed at Tess and flicked his hand away from himself and tossed his head. Reaching for his writing aide, he spelled out the word "pretty." I laughed and said, "It looks like you were flicking your hair like Tess." He giggled, nodded, and repeated the motion. This time, I saw that he was pretending to flick his (imaginary and long) hair in a flirtatious way. I copied his motion and flicked my own hair. Nick threw back his head and laughed, pointed at the horse, and flicked his imaginary hair once more.

While I wasn't able to elicit any reflective verbal answers from Nick, it was clear that he was connecting with Tess through this grooming activity and that he was experiencing something that was meaningful for him. If I had approached him with only my interpretation of what I initially thought he was experiencing, we may not have shared that joyful moment together.

In another EFL session with a similar group of students, we were focusing on improving social functioning skills in participants. The group consisted of mostly non-verbal students with cognitive, emotional, and physical challenges. Diagnoses ranged from cerebral palsy, autism, and Downs Syndrome. Two of the students were brothers who had been so severely neglected and abandoned by their parents that they had developed their own language of signs and sounds understood only between them. In designing this program, my co-facilitator and I decided to offer the students a sensory-based experience.

Using touch, sight, sound, smell, and breath, we introduced the students to the ways that horses use their senses. When I pointed out how one of the horses was sniffing us, two students immediately walked up to the horse and buried their faces into her. The teaching aide who had come with them offered one student his communication device after he had sniffed, and I asked him to tell us what that was like. "I smell to know her," he typed.

Because the students were allowed to make sense of their experiences, they were able to translate the learning into everyday life. In this instance, we were able to ask what they might do with one another to get to know one another better. We talked about what the human equivalent of sniffing is. They understood that sniffing was not a human way of greeting!

Chapter 6

Universal Themes of Life (and Death)

"We're all in this together"
~ Irv Yalom[1]

A few years ago, the Ad Council[2] set up a campaign called "Love Has No Labels," with the aim of illustrating that we all hold implicit biases, many of which we are unaware of. To emphasize this point, they set up giant X-ray screens in Santa Monica, California, on Valentine's Day, and asked real couples from different genders, ethnicities, and sexual orientations to dance, embrace, and/or kiss behind the screens, before revealing themselves. The sight of dancing skeletons drew a crowd, and the spontaneous reactions of passersby were caught on camera to highlight people's responses to those couples that surprised them: the inter-racial couple, the gay couple with a child, the hugging Imam and Rabbi, and the two women kissing and hugging, to name a few. The campaign was heartfelt and promoted acceptance and inclusion of all people across race, gender, sexual orientation, religion, age, and ability, and emphasized that underneath it all we are all human. This campaign went viral in 2015 and has continued since then in its various iterations to promote equality and inclusion for all.

On the surface, the Love has No Labels campaign sends a message of unity and equality, and yet there's something amiss in this for me. While I get the sentiment of the message, I do feel that there's a danger that the real struggles of people in minority groups might get missed. Without getting too much into the political sphere, for me it's akin to those who insist on using #alllivesmatter in response to #blacklivesmatter. There are differences, and those differences need to be acknowledged.

What I do appreciate about the campaign is that it gave some people a first glimpse into their own biases and challenged them to think about inclusion and diversity in a different way. I also believe that there are universal human *experiences* that transcend differences of race, gender, religion, sexual orientation, age, and ability. We *are* all human, and as such, we are all experiencing beings.

There are a few core themes that are foundational to human experiencing. In psychological terms, we call these themes "existential givens," a term coined by psychologist Irv Yalom. These givens are death, freedom, isolation, and meaninglessness.

We are broadly referring to human experiences as the need to be aware that death is a possibility, that we have the freedom to choose our own path, that we are a part of something or belong in some way, and that there is meaning in our life. These existential themes may show up in various ways during an equine-facilitated session, and while they may not be positioned or articulated in those words, we may be able to hear the deeper meaning with what clients/participants say or do. Holding the space with this framework allows us to focus on the core aim of any equine-facilitated session—that is, to facilitate more authentic relationships for our clients/participants, whatever the setting.

Death

Whether you are someone who has spent time contemplating what death means or not, you will have become aware at a young age that death exists. Yalom suggests that the knowledge that we exist now but that we will all one day cease to be creates an underlying anxiety that impacts the way we engage with the world around us. Perhaps you experienced the death of someone significant to you when you were young, and that has led you to keep your distance from people for fear of losing someone else. Perhaps you experienced losing a beloved pet and felt called to rescue all living creatures that come your way in a subconscious effort to replace the love that was lost. Death does not necessarily have to be a literal death. An ending, a loss—whether of life, relationships, hopes, dreams, and even material possessions—may spark feelings of anxiety or grief.

I know this process well. I was a curious child, the kind who would drive you crazy with questions, often landing on existential themes that were difficult for the adults around me to fathom, never mind explain to me. Like, when I overheard that someone had died in their sleep, I wanted to know how my body would know to wake me up in the morning? When will I know *inside* when it's time to die? If I can't remember someone anymore, does that mean that they've died? After being told that God guides us in everything we do, I had an image of humans as puppets and asked how many hands God has, and if someone dies, does he lose a set of hands? I was five at the time.

While I never lost anyone I loved through death as a young child, I was acutely aware of relational loss. Through the charitable work that my parents were involved in, I was aware of the realities of fostering and adoption from a very young age, and I attended boarding school from the age of nine. So I was particularly attuned to relational patterns of attachment in myself, and others. It was clear to me that I couldn't get attached quickly to people or places as the world was made of shifting sands, but once I did eventually let you in, you were in for life. This life in transition, of living in different countries, starting over and settling down only to up and move and start again, means that grief and loss were familiar ground. What I have learned, though, is that an awareness of death also brings life.

In the different client populations that we serve through equine-facilitated work, death as an existential given may show up in a number of ways. Whether it is literal death of a loved one—human or animal—or grief and loss in terms of relationship, health (cognitive, physical, or emotional), location, or culture, we have all experienced this process by virtue of being alive.

Balance

Rebecca found her way to me through a mutual friend and was looking for some mentoring and business coaching. Having recently completed a training program for equine-facilitated learning, she was feeling stuck in how she could move forward in the field. A lifelong horsewoman, Rebecca had been drawn to equine-facilitated work after attending a wilderness retreat where she experienced her first equine-facilitated learning session. She had recently moved onto her own ten-acre property, where she was hoping to launch her own program but felt that she wasn't getting anywhere. In our initial conversation on the phone, Rebecca had indicated that she wanted to work with me to explore how she could make this happen. As a mother whose youngest child had recently left home, she felt that this was the right time for her to turn her passion into a business.

During this particular session, Rebecca started by saying that she wanted to work with Freeman, a bay Morgan gelding with whom she

had connected previously. As we walked out to the field towards the
herd, Freeman lifted his head and looked in our direction.

> **Rebecca:** Ha! He's already looking at us and wondering what
> we want from him.
> **Me:** What's that like for you?
> **Rebecca:** Oh, I get it. There's always something isn't there?
> Always someone or something wanting something from you.
> **Me:** What do you want from him?
> **Rebecca:** I don't want anything from him really. I just want
> to get a bit closer. I feel like we're too far away.

As we continued to walk towards the herd, Freeman dropped his
head momentarily before turning away from us and walking across
to the other side of the paddock. The rest of the herd followed him.
Rebecca stopped in her tracks.

> **Me:** What's happening for you right now?
> **Rebecca:** I don't think they want me to get any closer. They
> seem quite happy doing their own thing without me intruding.

Rebecca let out a deep sigh.

> **Me:** What does this mean for you?
> **Rebecca:** It just reminds me of my kids; they don't need their
> mama anymore, and I feel so disconnected from them. They've
> all moved out of town, so it's not easy to see them. That's why
> I thought I'd get started with this business, so I can keep
> myself busy without intruding on them so much. But I can't
> just switch from being a mom to being a businesswoman
> overnight! Like, how do I let go of being a mom?

Rebecca sighed again, turned her back to the horses, folded her
arms across her chest, and looked down at the ground. The horses
turned to face us from across the pasture. In that moment, I imagined
that Rebecca was struggling in her business not so much with the
practicalities of how to launch, but more with her transition from
one season of life to another, an existential death that needed to be
attended to.

Me: I see you've turned so that the horses are behind you. What are you experiencing right now?

Rebecca: I see space in front of me, like I'm supposed to step forward into it, but there's so much of it that it feels too overwhelming.

Me: What about the horses?

Rebecca (looking over her shoulder): Oh! They're all standing there looking at us.

Me: What's it like to see them do that?

Rebecca (turning to face the herd): It's nice. Like they're acknowledging I'm here, but I don't have to be right there with them.

Me: What meaning does that have for you?

Rebecca: I've been feeling like I've needed to turn my back on my life as a stay-at-home mom and a role I've lived for so long in order to get going with my business. But I guess it doesn't have to be all or nothing! It's not like I'll ever stop being a mom. I suppose I've always had the privilege of choosing to stay home, so it was either work or be a mom, not both. But I can have both, right?

We continued with the session, exploring how it felt for Rebecca to move around the paddock, to experience her proximity and distance from the herd. At each position she chose, I asked her what she was experiencing, how connected (or not) she felt to the horses. Through moving around the paddock, Rebecca was able to experience herself in relation to the horses in different ways. From each vantage point, I asked her to name something that she wanted to let go of, keep, or hold loosely. As Rebecca picked her positions, the horses began to spread out around the paddock. Freeman walked over and stood with her briefly before continuing on his way.

Rebecca picked a spot in the middle of the paddock and stood looking around her. Freeman had wandered over to the fence line but had turned and was grazing while facing her. The two mares in the herd were standing under a tree, heads low and taking a nap.

One of the other geldings, Jacob, began to walk towards Rebecca, stopping about ten feet away. Slowly, he stepped closer, pausing after each step. Jacob stretched his neck out and nudged Rebecca on her shoulder, dropped his head to graze at her feet, and then stretched out and nudged her again. Rebecca giggled and reached her hand up to scratch his neck. Jacob nudged her again.

Rebecca: I think he wants me to move!
Me: What would you like to do?
Rebecca: I guess I can move if he wants

Rebecca took a step forward. Jacob followed and nudged her again. Rebecca took another step forward and looked over her shoulder. Jacob followed. Slowly, they started to walk together around the paddock, with Rebecca occasionally stopping, and Jacob following. They meandered around the paddock for a few minutes before returning to the center.

Rebecca: That was amazing! He just followed me every which way I went!!
Me: What does that mean for you?
Rebecca: Well, I noticed that Freeman was over there and that wherever I went, I could still see him. Jacob just followed and trusted wherever I went would be fine. I feel like I can focus on both of them, like maybe I can focus on family *and* launching this business. I just need to remember to find that balance where I can do both. Maybe, I can let go of my fear of disconnection with my kids and keep them in mind even when I'm doing my own thing.

Rebecca's experience in this equine-facilitated session supported her to transition from the shift of being focused on her children's needs to attending to her own. Her journey was one of recognizing that change and growth necessitate letting go. While we never articulated this process in sessions as an existential death, this theme reappeared throughout our time together. Focusing more on her passion and needs meant sacrificing time and energy for other things. In reaching for her dreams, there was an acknowledgment of the end of an era and the beginning of another. The anxiety that she had felt, which had manifested as feeling stuck and an inability to move forward, was replaced by a sense of gratitude for the privilege of having had the choice to be a stay-at-home mom, and created the desire to step into the unknown with her business plans.

The paradoxical nature of the acceptance of death as part of our human existence is that it often lends itself to the unleashing of life force. It is not surprising that when people experience a near-death incident, they will frequently respond with the realization that life is short and seek to fulfill their life's passions and goals, reconnect with loved ones, and become more focused on the present moment. As Yalom says, "The integrations of the idea of death saves us; rather than sentence us to existences of terror or bleak pessimism, it acts as a catalyst to plunge us into more authentic life modes, and it enhances our pleasure in the living of life."

A few years ago, I experienced something similar to this wake-up call through an unexpected gift from a man I knew as "Mr. Bill."

Mr. Bill's Last Gift

While working at a therapeutic riding center in Ohio, I had the privilege of working with an army of volunteers who supported the program by dedicating their time and energy into ensuring that the horses were well cared for and that the students had safe and enjoyable lessons. By walking alongside the horse and rider during the lesson, volunteers often develop strong attachments to the students they work with, and vice versa.

"Mr. Bill" was one of our first volunteers in the program. From the very beginning, he walked alongside Georgia—a bright, beautiful, and chatty "four, almost five-year-old" student. When Georgia was anxious, he would calm her, distracting her with questions about her day, her favorite color or toy. When she lost focus while riding, Mr. Bill would redirect her attention and guide her through the task at hand. For 18 months, Mr. Bill was a solid presence in Georgia's weekly lessons. Sometimes, she would arrive for her lesson at the end of a particularly tough week, unwilling to provide anything more than monosyllabic answers, until Mr. Bill coaxed her out of her shell, and she would transform before our eyes into the bubbly, giggly child we recognized. Their relationship warmed my heart; their mutual love and adoration was a joy to behold.

Mr. Bill passed away on December 29, 2014 after fighting for his life for two weeks from the trauma caused as a result of a senseless tragedy that devastated two families and left the rest of us who knew Mr. Bill in shock. After the accident, there was a tremendous outpouring of support, love, and care for the family as our barn community pulled together to provide emotional and practical support: organizing a schedule for delivering meals to the hospital as he lay in intensive care, offering rides to appointments for his children so his wife could stay by his side, collecting donations for

Christmas gifts, and taking turns to sit with the family as they waited and prayed for his recovery.

What took me by surprise wasn't the community's response to the tragedy, but how much a part of the community I realized I had become. Due to my husband's job, I'd been living a relatively nomadic life for a few years, moving through countries, states, and cities. As someone who loathes small talk and the "getting to know you" phase of relationships, this lifestyle had been challenging for me. It takes me a while to adjust to my surroundings, figure out with whom I can let my guard down, and find a sense of belonging. I feel like I usually have a good gut feel of where and how I fit within groups and organizations that I join and am sensitive to boundaries that need to be softened or held firm. Up until that moment, I had situated myself at the periphery of this community, not through lack of desire to belong but through fear of becoming too attached.

Mr. Bill's unassuming, humble, and loyal presence had touched many lives and as the tragedy unfolded, it became clear to me that our "barn family" was responding to this event in the way that Mr. Bill lived his life: through selfless service to others, and with love, respect, and integrity. Belonging to this family meant taking responsibility and care for others and, above all, being present wholeheartedly.

As Mr. Bill took a turn for the worse and the community pulled together to comfort each other and offer strength to his family, I was flooded with appreciation for having a place within this incredible group of people who had welcomed me with open arms. Recognizing my fear of attachment as an anticipation of grief allowed me to surrender into the comforting arms of this community. In much the same way as Mr. Bill would coax young Georgia out of her shell, the message was clear: be here now and find joy through connection because we can never anticipate what comes next. While grief may become reality, should my nomadic existence or other events intervene the joy of connection in the moment was worth the risk.

I am proud to be counted as part of this barn family despite no longer being in Ohio and know that Mr. Bill's legacy lives on in that program. Whenever I think of him and the joy that he brought to so many, I am filled with deep gratitude for this lesson, his last gift to me, and honored beyond measure for having been graced by his presence.

Freedom

What does freedom mean to you? Being able to do whatever you want without constraints? Or perhaps it elicits feelings of patriotism, and the idea that freedom is always paired with sacrifice? Is freedom always desirable? Or is it a burden that one must bear? Do you believe in fate or destiny? How does that factor into your sense of freedom and personal agency?

Freedom, as an existential given, refers to the responsibility one must take in one's own life. This is challenging, and often a tough pill to swallow. We can think of freedom as choice, and while we might appreciate the privilege of having choice, the process of actually choosing may be fraught with difficulty. It is this tension between taking responsibility for our own actions through intentional choice and believing that we are constrained in what choices are available that often presents itself as a place of inaction in our participants.

I remember when I first moved to the United States and went to the grocery store to stock up on some essentials. We had literally just arrived and moved into our temporary accommodation the day before. This wasn't the first time I'd visited the States; I'd spent many summers visiting family in California, so I wasn't expecting to experience much of a culture shock. What I hadn't experienced, though, was day-to-day living as an adult, so I was certainly not expecting the discombobulating experience of walking into the biggest grocery store I had ever seen. Compared to the relatively small supermarkets in the UK, this particular store seemed enormous to me. I recognize now that it was an average-sized US grocery store, but at the time it seemed enormous.

I remember walking through aisle after aisle, pushing my shopping cart—which I learned quickly not to call a trolley—trying to remember what I needed. Turning down the cereal aisle, I thought that some good old-fashioned oatmeal might help me feel more at home. Yes, that should do the trick. Quaker Oats, plain and simple, nice and cozy, will give me a taste of home, I thought.

I looked up and was confronted by a dazzling display of oatmeal. Row upon row of different flavors—cinnamon and apple, strawberries and cream, peanut butter, banana—and so many varieties—steel cut, instant, organic, quick-cook, and Paleo. My brain froze, and I was rooted to the spot. I literally had no idea how to proceed. I must have stood staring at those shelves for a good fifteen minutes before turning around and walking out of the store. It was just too overwhelming in that moment.

I can now recall this incident with humor, but at the time my experience was one of confusion and anxiety. Freedom, for many, means having the ability to choose for themselves, and within the United States, it also often equates to the idea that the more choice we have the better. Sheena Lyengar,[3] a professor at Columbia Business School, talks about the myth that the more choices we have, the more likely we'll make the right choice. Lyengar says that, in fact, the opposite is true, and that when we are faced with too many choices, we can become overwhelmed and get stuck.

Conversely, many people feel a yearning for freedom when choices are not as abundant. From young professionals who want to be financially independent but cannot afford to rent a place alone and feel stuck living with their parents, to chief executives of major corporations who feel trapped in the rat race in order to provide their families the standard of living they are accustomed to, being accountable for the choice of comfort over relative hardship can be a bitter pill to swallow. The young professional could move out and live in a shared house. It may not be ideal and may not be what they had hoped for, but it would be a step towards the financial independence and freedom they yearn for; however, it also comes with the sacrifice of comfort and familiarity. The chief executive could choose to leave and take a lesser paying job, but that comes with potential shame, judgment, and loss of status and relationships. And so we arrive at the same point of feeling stuck as when our choices feel too abundant.

Dolan Cummings,[4] social and political commentator and author of *The Existential Leap*, says:

> The key thing is that existential freedom cannot be denied or withheld, only disavowed. It is disavowed when we refuse to acknowledge that we have a choice and insist that our actions are determined by our circumstances, whether these are external or even just part of our own background.

In this way, freedom, as an existential given, is the process by which we acknowledge the enormity of the choices we have, the courage it sometimes takes to make a choice, and the risk of making the wrong one.

Isolation

If freedom is an existential given and we are responsible for our own choices, then it follows that in that aloneness we will feel the existential given of isolation. This is not to say that we cannot engage in deep, meaningful relationships, but that we are so wired to need connection that we will always feel the threat of isolation and not belonging. Existential psychologist Rollo May[5] referred to this as our constant awareness of being a part of, or apart from, our situational context.

How connected, or disconnected, we are in each moment can bring up feelings of belonging or not belonging. Within any cultural context, awareness of difference can bring about feelings of isolation. How do we maintain a sense of aloneness enough to become an individual without losing connection altogether? How do we join in and belong without conforming and losing our sense of self? Brené Brown[6] talks about the difference between belonging and conforming: "Belonging is being accepted for you. Fitting in, is being accepted for being like everyone else...I get to be me if I belong. I have to be like you to fit in."

Within an equine-facilitated session, the physical and emotional shifts that clients/participants demonstrate will often highlight issues of belonging and isolation. How they position themselves in relation to each other, and in relation to the horses, may have some significance in where they see themselves within the group.

Connecting Across the Divide

A few years ago, I ran an EFL session with a team of sales directors of a US-based national retail company. The eight participants were each responsible for a regional team of between 20 and 50 sales staff spread across the country. Most of the interactions that they had with their staff were via online communication—video conferencing, emails, and texts. While their contact with one another was mostly online, they met their regional team managers on a weekly, face-to-face basis; however, they would often not have in-person contact with the customer-facing sales teams whom these regional team managers were responsible for, other than at quarterly meetings. The company had recently undergone a restructuring process, and a large number of employees had been laid off. In conducting the needs analysis, the human resources director had mentioned that the team was very fragmented and wanted the equine-facilitated session to provide a team-building experience for the eight sales directors.

As the participants arrived, I noticed that they were all very high energy, loud, and frantic. They constantly checked their cell phones, and a couple of them had walked into the barn still talking on their phones. They were talking to each other loudly, joking around, and ribbing each other about their monthly sales figures. It took a little while to get them to settle, and after our initial meet and greet, safety protocol, and general introduction to the day's agenda, I led the participants in a herd-observation exercise.

Working with three horses, I asked the participants to observe the horses in silence. The horses were in a small paddock and full of energy, trotting around the paddock, bucking and kicking. At the sight of the participants approaching, they all rushed over to the gate, pausing momentarily before galloping off to charge around the paddock. The group spread themselves out along the fence line, taking up the full length of the paddock, so that it was difficult to address them all without raising my voice. A few of the participants had taken a few steps back away from the fence. Checking in with the group, I asked what they were experiencing. One participant said, "They're quite intimidating, aren't they? I can feel the ground shaking when they're charging around." Another one commented that they loved the sound of hooves hitting the ground. Someone else commented that they could see that the horses were having a good time and looked excited by having visitors.

I knew from my needs analysis that this team might be experiencing some fragmentation, so I was curious about how they had spread themselves out along the fence line. I also noticed that although the horses were running around and full of energy, they were doing this in a synchronized manner with one another; as one turned, the others followed, and they moved as one unit.

Me: I notice that you are all spread out along the fence line. What's it like for you to be observing the horses from where you are?
Group member 1: I'm fascinated by how they're able to move so fast without bumping into each other
Group member 2 (laughing): I'm assuming that we spread out so that we could see better, but I guess that makes it difficult for us to talk to each other!

Me: So there's something here about spreading out and not bumping into one another. How does that relate to your work environment?

This question opened up a discussion on how important it was for each of them to be clear about their boundaries in terms of sales territories, and that in order to avoid any confusion or conflict regarding commissions, they had learned to defend their territories. This created a culture of competition rather than collaboration, where information might not be shared to assist another team's sales in case the forwarding of such information led to clients being "poached" by a neighboring region.

As the team began to open up about their experiences, they had all organically moved closer together in order to be able to hear each other. In the meantime, the horses had stopped running around and were grazing in close proximity to one another. I drew attention to this process and asked the team what they were experiencing in that moment and to notice what they might want from the horses and/or one another.

One participant commented that they were enjoying watching how the horses shared their space (or "territory") and drew an analogy of the abundance of grass available as sales opportunities. Others expressed a desire to get closer to the horses or wanting the horses to come over to the fence. This opened up an opportunity for the team to talk about how difficult it was for them to acknowledge when they wanted more connection with one another and with their staff members. In an environment in which the organization was going through a major restructure, there was a pervading sense that requests for support would be seen as a weakness that might place themselves at risk of being expendable. So it was safer to go it alone.

I invited the group to work together to figure out how they could enter into the space with the horses and stay "connected" in some way. I offered them the use of any of the props that they could find available in the paddock (lunge lines, lead rope, cones, ground poles, hula-hoops, barrels etc.). After a brief strategy meeting, the group decided to place four ground poles in a square in the middle of the paddock for them to stand inside. During the process of the group deciding where they wanted to place this square, the horses continued to graze nearby.

Once they had situated themselves within the square, I asked the group to pay attention to their individual inclinations as to who, where, and how they felt pulled towards in relation to one another and the horses. Checking in with what they were experiencing, a few of the participants expressed that they now felt trapped and disconnected. One participant noticed that this was contrary to how he thought he'd feel. Standing together in the square would, he thought, bring them together, but he now felt that he had no choice —that he *had* to be inside the square rather than wanting to be. Another participant noticed that she also wanted to step outside the square and move towards the horses but felt that she had to stay with everyone else and likened it to how it feels working remotely with her staff members. I asked the group to reflect on these comments and invited them to figure out a way where individuality could be expressed while still maintaining connection within the group—and also create a more intentional connection with the horses.

By tracking the process as it unfolded, the participants were able to articulate moment by moment, what was significant for them in their experience. By supporting the connections between the participants and the horses, we were able to co-create an experience for the group that led to each member taking turns to step outside the square while holding on to a "lifeline" of connection via a lunge line as they approached the horses to meet and greet them. The horses were given the freedom to come and go as they wished, allowing the participants to experience the choices that were available to everyone involved.

In this scenario, the fragmented nature of the team brought up existential issues related to freedom and isolation. Company restructuring will often raise uncertainty and feelings of lack of choice. The decision to stay in a role that could potentially disappear and wait for the choice to be made for you, or jump ship into the unknown and risk not being able to find alternative employment, is tough. The geographical nature of their roles brought up issues of isolation. In noticing the energy, positioning, and ways of communication within the group, as well as the horses' energy and movement, the herd observation highlighted some key themes for them.

Through bringing awareness to how the team had spread themselves out along the fence line, we were able to address some of these feelings of choice and isolation and create an experience that allowed the participants to make those choices in real time to foster a clear sense of belonging, while still remaining authentic to their individual process.

As with any session, there were a hundred different ways that the process may have emerged. I could have picked up, right from the start, the feeling of intimidation that one participant felt and inquired about that more in the context of a cut-throat sales environment, where the old saying that "You're only as good as your last sale" still prevails and competition is more common than collaboration. Given the energy levels of the team and of the horses, I could have reiterated safety concerns while in the paddock with the horses. This may have brought up issues around risk, and how that plays out at work. Finding out how participants experience the organization and team culture can also be a key to linking the learning into their everyday world. By attending to the here and now, what and how, and I–Thou of the session, the team was able to leave with an embodied experience of what it was like to be in connection with one another and take that learning back into the workplace.

Meaninglessness

There is no greater gift you can give or receive than to honor your calling. It's why you were born, and how you become most truly alive. ~ Oprah Winfrey

We are meaning-making creatures. We each hold within us an innate desire to understand the reason for our existence. Much like the existential given of death, the time at which our existential meaninglessness dawns upon us will vary from one person to the next. Some may ponder these existential questions from a young age, and others may not be hit with the full force of it until middle age (often culminating in a so-called "mid-life crisis"). Meaninglessness may manifest in a lack of purpose, or the feeling of helplessness in the face of our immediate circumstances (linked to existential freedom), or our inability to step into a more authentic way of being in the world by aligning ourselves with our sense of integrity and our sense of existential purpose.

Having shared with you my death anxiety as a child, it will come as no surprise to you that as a child I was also particular concerned with the "why" of all things. Why are we here? Why are we doing this? Why does this matter? Why was I born? My questions also concerned the lack of evidence for the answers I was given, in the form of "But how do you *know*?" For me, the lived experience and meaning made by another was often out of sync with my own lived experience and the meaning I made. I saw contradictions in the world around me and experienced statements made as facts that were contrary to my understanding. So, amid this confusion, I found strange solace in questioning the meaning of life and death. This is not something that I have ever grown out of either.

I have found, though, that it is this desire to question everything that has allowed me to become crystal clear as to what I give meaning to in my life. There's a Japanese concept called *ikigai*. It means your reason for being, your inner most sense of why you exist and what brought you here. Not what we feel we should do or what we need to do in order to get the bills paid, or what we think we are good at, but the combination of what the world needs—our talents, our potential, passion, and values. Dan Buettner[7], award-winning journalist and author of *The Blue Zones*, researched the secrets to a long and healthy life and brought the concept of ikigai into Western cultural awareness.

The term *ikigai* (pronounced ee-key-guy) comprises two Japanese words: *iki,* referring to life, and *gai*, which roughly means "the realization of what one expects and hopes for. Ikigai is seen as the convergence of four primary elements:

- What you love (your passion)
- What the world needs (your mission)
- What you are good at (your vocation)
- What you can get paid for (your profession)

The word *ikigai*, the intersection of these four elements, is seen as the source of value or what make one's life truly worthwhile. When we are not living in line with our ikigai, or when we don't allow ourselves to stretch for what we know in our bones is what we are on this Earth to be and what makes us feel truly alive, feelings of malaise, emptiness, uncertainty, dissatisfaction, and health issues may arise. In the words of Viktor Frankl[8], author of *Mans' Search for Meaning* and founder of an existential psychology movement known as Logotherapy, "Those who have a 'why' to live, can bear with almost any 'how'." As a Holocaust survivor, Frankl drew strength and sustenance from his theory that in any given circumstance, if we can find the meaning behind the experience, then we can endure its suffering: "If there is meaning in life at all, then there must be meaning in suffering."

Many of us come into this work as equine-facilitated practitioners because of our love of horses and our belief that they can offer solace, healing, and learning to others in a way that we have experienced personally. Many of us have experienced deep shifts in our own process and confronted our demons through these existential givens. We may have suffered and sacrificed, endured and survived to arrive at a place where we feel called to offer our services to fellow travelers on this journey called life. So we step into this space from a deep sense of knowing, with a desire and yearning to share these experiences with others. And when we witness the connections made, and learning gained, and wholeness restored to those we serve, we know in our bones that we are in the right place and that we have found our ikigai.

Existential Givens: Self-Reflection

Now that we've reestablished "why" we feel called to do this work, it's important for us to dig a little deeper into how self-reflection is critical to how we facilitate sessions within an equine-facilitated context.

When thinking about running a session, what are the questions that emerge for you most often? Notice what happens to you physically. All emotions begin with physical sensations and as energy in motion through our bodies. Take a breath and check-in with your bodily self. Now, imagine you are about to facilitate a session for your chosen client population. It may be a group that you are familiar with, a weekly or monthly group with varying members who already know each other; or it may be a brand-new program with clients/participants who have never met before. It may be a group that you've run multiple times or a new idea that you are piloting. It may be the very first session you'll facilitate. Whatever it may be, take a breath and really immerse yourself into visualizing the setting of this group.

Now, take a few moments to write down the questions you are asking yourself. Sink into the experience of what it might be like to step in front of this particular group. Imagine the horses that you will be partnering with. What questions come to mind?

Taking a look at your questions, I'm guessing that we can group them into the following general categories:

- Doing
- Being
- Fears
- Hopes

You may find yourself questioning whether you have the knowledge, skills, or ability to run a "successful" session. It may be that you are thinking of what to "do" with your clients/participants, in terms of activities or tasks, and how they might respond to these. It may be that you are anxious about how to engage them in the session, or if you are able to meet them where they're at. You may find yourself imagining what impact your session will have. It may be that you are focusing on whether the horses will respond in the way that you'd hoped. Whatever your thoughts and feelings are about this process, it's important for you to notice what emerges and how this might impact your ability to stay present with your clients/participants in that moment. These are the moments where we are pulled away from our sense of ikigai.

In my first book, I referred to contemporary philosopher and writer Mark Rowlands[9], who says that the only difference between humans and all other animals is that humans believe the stories they tell themselves. I remind myself of this often; I find it to be a comforting reality check that whatever is going on in my head may not be what is actually emerging in front of me. Our self-reflective process and examination of the questions that we are challenging ourselves with allow us to notice the stories we may tell ourselves about what is happening in the moment, and provides information on how we might be disconnecting from our clients/participants in sessions. Remembering that everything that we do is in an effort to support relationships, during the session with and between our clients/participants, ourselves, and our horses, how do these stories interrupt our ability to meet the other where they're at?

Imposter Syndrome

By increasing our awareness of the ways in which we interrupt our own ability to maintain connection, we can find ways to support ourselves to stay fully present. At the HERD Institute, we emphasize the importance of holding a compassionate approach to working with our horses. Self-compassion is equally important.

The most common struggle for practitioners, particularly in the early stages, is a sense of Imposter Syndrome. Clinical psychologists

Pauline Clance and Suzanne Imes [10] introduced this term in the 1970s. It refers to an individual's internalized fear of being found out to be a "fraud." Despite evidence to the contrary that indicates we are competent in the area ,we feel we're lacking; our internalized fear tells us the story that we are not good enough. Whenever we step outside our comfort zone or compare ourselves with others and find ourselves lacking, we question whether we have what it takes, whether we have the knowledge or skills that we need. While the experience of this can range from being utterly debilitating or a small niggling doubt, or somewhere in between, it pulls us away from the reality of our skill set and knocks our confidence.

What's interesting about this phenomenon is that everyone experiences it in some form and at some point in our lives. One of the ways that we can combat our self-doubt, or how we get in our own way, is to take note of Brené Brown's research on shame and vulnerability. We can accept that to be seen is to be vulnerable, to be vulnerable is courageous, and that courage is contagious. In those moments, we can remind ourselves that our role as facilitators is not about being the expert in the arena; it's about showing up fully to be present with our clients/participants. We can also build our network and community so that we have a soft place to land, to share our struggles, and to recharge so that we can rise to the challenge once more.

Chapter 7

Relational Ethics

In the early '90s, UK-based wood-dye manufacturing company Ronseal [1] launched an advertising campaign to demystify its products. The first commercial showed a man painting a fence and then watching it dry. Ronseal wanted to highlight the fact that while not all products provided a glamorous outcome, these everyday moments were essential and that their product "Does exactly what it says on the tin." This idiom is now embedded in English culture to convey the astonishing effectiveness of something presented authentically and to good effect.

We are in the business of relationships—the support, development, and repair of relationships in order to offer our clients and participants a more authentic and meaningful way to connect with others in their lives. We choose to do this in partnership with horses, relying on their innate ability to respond authentically in each moment to all of us, and believing that they can offer powerful insights into how we relate to others. We are committed to honoring our horses as equal partners in this process, acknowledging that we have our own distinct relationships with each of the horses we work with, all of which impacts the contextual fabric of the services we provide.

In order to hold our integrity within this frame of reference, we need to address the relational ethics of how we conduct our equine-facilitated work. We need to understand that this is not only a cursory glance or token gesture towards meeting our ethical standards, but the starting point in how we interact with all of our equine partners. Remember that HERD stands for Human–Equine Relational Development, so this message is at the heart of our approach. Human–Equine Relational Development is the business that we are in. Let's make sure we do exactly what it says on the tin.

What is Relational Ethics?

Relational ethics as a discipline is a contemporary approach to ethics that emphasizes ethical action as a contextual dynamic. It represents the complex process through which decisions and interactions that impact a relationship are considered and acted upon. Bergum and Dossetor[2] from the University of Alberta, Canada, and authors of the book *Relational Ethics: The Full Meaning of Respect,* outline four key elements within the concept of relational ethics:

- Mutual respect
- Engagement
- Embodied knowledge
- Environment

Mutual respect is identified as the core theme of relational ethics and defined as an inter-subjective and reciprocal process that emphasizes acceptance of difference. Mutual respect is both respecting the other and oneself.

Engagement is offered as an invitation to step alongside the other and implores the cultivation of authentic connection. It calls upon practitioners to offer themselves wholly through presence, compassion, and empathy.

Embodied knowledge is a reminder that we are multi-dimensional beings that operate not only through rational thought. When we bring ourselves into connection with the fullness of our body and mind, we can allow for a more authentic relationship. Within embodied knowledge, we can give equal status to heart and mind.

Environment is offered as a reminder that we are all connected beyond our immediate selves, expanding the concept of the relational space to include the full context of each person's lived experience and situation within the world in which we live. It encompasses a worldview of interconnectedness, acknowledging that there is no self without another, and that we are all part of an inter-dependent, complex system.

I was delighted when I first came across Bergum and Dossetor's work. Their positioning of what I had organically labeled relational ethics in my own mind matched so well with the philosophical foundations behind the HERD models of equine-facilitated work. These four tenets of relational ethics were already embedded within

The HERD Institute's Codes of Ethics and Professional Practice. Our philosophical foundations of awareness of self, other, environment; our quest for connection and relationships through an authentic and embodied process; and our emphasis on I–Thou ways of relating fit beautifully into this framework.

While Bergum and Dossetor's work refers to the relational ethics of working in a human healthcare context, I believe that these principles can be easily transposed into our work within an equine-facilitated environment. Taking these four tenets and applying them to our clients, participants, and horses, allows us to truly integrate an ethical framework into our practice.

Relational Ethics in Practice

Within the equine industry, the word "respect" is often bandied around as an expectation in our interactions with horses—mostly with reference to whether the horse is respectful of the human or not. We talk about horses pushing our boundaries or not respecting our space. We emphasize the need to teach them how to back up and move their feet, apparently because that's what horses do to each other. In this context, the meaning of "respect" has morphed into something that comes from a human place of dominance, control, and fear.

From a relational ethics perspective, we need to ask ourselves whether this is a version of "respect" that we actually want to foster and, well, respect. Where is the mutuality in this process?

I came into the field of equine-facilitated work as a seasoned organizational trainer, coach, and psychotherapist, with relatively little horse experience. I was fortunate enough to share my journey with a close friend, Elisabeth (Lis) Crabtree, who is a lifelong horsewoman. We spent many hours talking about how to "translate" therapeutic relational principles to the way we work with horses. Many times when I felt stuck in my relationship with the horses, I would turn to Lis and ask, "What would you do?" Her response was always, "What would you do if this was one of your therapy clients?" Lis didn't ask this of me with the assumption that I was treating my horses as needing therapy, but from the knowledge that I approached therapy from an existential—humanistic and Gestalt perspective that honored the "other" by accepting them as they are. These conversations helped to shape the type of practitioner I wanted to be with my horses. I wanted to work with them on an equal footing as much as possible, recognizing them as sentient beings in their own right, with their own ways of being in the world, with their own cognitive understanding, emotions, and physicality that was different yet also still recognizable. I wanted to foster mutuality in our experiencing of each other.

A couple of years ago, I stumbled across a book that reconnected me deeply to my initial intentions and echoed the conversations I'd had with Lis. The book, *Equus Lost* by De Giorgio and De Giorgio-Schoorl,[3] is based on approaching horses from a zooanthropological perspective.

With the increase in attention towards the study of human–animal bonds and interactions, there is now more awareness of the intricacies of how humans relate to non-human animals situated in their own species-specific worlds and cultures. Zooanthropology is the study of these relational dynamics, with theoretical concepts that can be applied to our day-to-day interactions in order to promote well-being for *both* human and animal. Zooanthropology is rooted in the field of cognitive ethology, where animals are seen as individual, sentient beings, with awareness and cognitive abilities. What I like about this approach is that it's one thing to say that we will treat our equine partners with respect, dignity, and compassion, and another to actively engage them in ways that promote their well-being, transforming intention into action. What I love about De Giorgio's writing, too, is that his philosophy towards horses can also be applied to humans. For example, he says, "instead of a reaction to something, behavior should be interpreted and understood as the way an experience is lived and perceived."

And yes, he's talking about horses here. But isn't that what we also are striving for with humans? This fits into the HERD model's phenomenological way of relating, where we maintain an active curiosity about the meaning our participants make of their experiences in each moment.

But what does this look like in practice within the context of equine-facilitated work? If mutual respect is defined as an inter-subjective and reciprocal process that emphasizes acceptance of difference, then we need to clarify what we mean by that. How can we foster human–equine relational development through a mutually respectful process?

For me, in any discussion on ethics, it is essential to give consideration to issues of diversity. With regard to horses, we are challenged to question human–equine practices and beliefs that may have been ingrained in us from the moment we fell in love with horses. We may need to challenge these beliefs and consider alternative ways of understanding our horses' experiences, perhaps from a less human-centric point of view.

With regard to humans, we need to encourage practitioners to pay *active* attention and be sensitive to differences in socio-economics, race, ethnicity, education, class, gender, sexuality, physical abilities, and neurodiversity. It is not enough to pay lip service to these concepts from a majority perspective. Practitioners must possess the self-awareness and motivation to seek out their own blind spots in these issues so that they can truly engage the other with mutual respect.

In 1998, a group of scientists from Harvard University, the University of Washington, and the University of Virginia got together to form Project Implicit. [4] This non-profit organization works collaboratively across an international network of researchers to investigate implicit social cognition—i.e., thoughts and emotions that are mostly outside of conscious awareness.

Project Implicit has been a pioneering force behind challenging attitudes, stereotypes, and hidden biases that impact the way we perceive others and make decisions within relationships. Its aim is to bring "academic research into practical applications for addressing diversity, improving decision-making, and increasing the likelihood that practices are aligned with personal and organizational values." By partnering with Harvard University, Project Implicit has created online assessment tools to highlight areas of implicit bias.

These assessments are a part of The HERD Institute curriculum, as they fall in line with our commitment of actively attending to personal awareness. The assessments are free, and I would highly recommend anyone to go and try them out. What I'm fascinated by is how people respond to them—from how they view the idea of taking them, how they interact with the tests themselves, and how they react to the results. I find it interesting that there are still so many students coming into this work who believe that they "don't hold any biases," or admit to trying to "give the correct answers," or who react defensively against the results given by criticizing the format of the tests. As if the idea that we hold any biases at all means that we are not evolved enough as human beings, so we have to defend ourselves from that notion and feel that the inherent aim is to be completely judgment and bias free.

I'd like to take this opportunity to debunk that particular myth right here, right now. Because it is a myth. It is a myth that we can operate without bias, because we are biologically, environmentally, and socially primed for it. We are meaning-making creatures, remember? This means that all of our experiences will shape who we are in each moment and impact the way that we respond and react in any given situation. Yes, we can absolutely attend to the fact that certain experiences and teachings we've been exposed to will influence the way we think and behave. Yes, it is possible for us to shine a light on them and challenge whether we agree with these values and beliefs. It is not possible, however, to walk through this life being completely bias free.

In any case, the aim is not to erase all of our biases, but instead to acknowledge that we all have unconscious biases and need to work to raise our awareness of them. By bringing these biases to light, we can actively choose and reflect on our thoughts and actions from a different lens. We ALL have biases as a result of being alive in a relational space; our environment, our culture, our upbringing, our experiences, and our own choices speak volumes about how we have become who we are. Stepping into an equine-facilitated setting with the intention to be aware of our biases so that we can interact with our participants and horses with intentional non-judgment helps us to provide a safe space for our participants.

We can also bring this intention to our beliefs and values in how we relate to our equine partners by challenging some "givens" within the industry. Some questions for you to consider might be:

1. What do you believe about domesticated horses and herd dynamics?
2. What are your thoughts on pressure-and-release training methods?
3. How do you feel about working horses in a round pen?
4. What are your opinions on natural horsemanship methods of "join up"?
5. What type of tack do you use, and why?
6. What choice do you give your horses when it comes to whether they work or not?
7. Is it okay to ride horses?
8. Are we exploiting the horses in our care by asking them to work with us?
9. What are your beliefs about shoeing and trimming?

10. How much turnout time is optimum for your horse?

Some of these questions will challenge us to think more critically of things that we may have always taken for granted and may require us to sit in some discomfort. Some of them might emphasize how we may not have questioned enough of what we have learned. The aim here is not to position ourselves in a "right" or "wrong" paradigm, but to increase our awareness of any inconsistencies in our philosophy and practice while acknowledging that we have choices and personal agency in terms of how we want to engage in these relationships moving forward.

I remember a few years ago, when I was in the midst of my doctoral program and struggling through an assignment on ethics, in a moment of clarity I realized that I had never really challenged what I had been taught with regard to how to interact with horses, that I'd taken for granted that there was only one way of communicating. A question began to form in my mind: What if everything I've ever been taught about horsemanship was rooted only in a white man's perspective?"

I literally crumpled under the weight of that question, not because the answer might have been "Yes, it's true," but that it had never even occurred to me to ask the question previously. I went down a deep rabbit hole that day that involved me asking a hundred more questions, such as "Do horses living in different cultures behave differently?" and "Do horses experience breed preferences and, if so, is that akin to racism?" or "Do all horses speak the same language because they are one species, or do they learn different ways to communicate that are breed or country specific?"

I basically blew up my brain that day. And while I don't have the answers (yet) to all of those questions, it was an important step in my evolution as someone who partners with horses to acknowledge the need to critically assess the what and how of my fundamental beliefs and my personal ethics in relation to these majestic creatures. I want to recognize that we all arrive at this point on our journey in differing degrees, and while some of you may be further along on this journey than I am, I want to invite you to continue to ask the question, "How can I engage with my equine partners in a manner that is consistent with my values?" In this way, we can ensure that we are practicing clear relational ethics grounded in mutual respect and engagement.

Embodying Relational Ethics

Having questioned some of what I had previously taken for granted as truths, I was able to understand with hindsight how mismatched my embodied experience of a situation was compared to what I was being told. When I first started working with horses as an adult, after having not been around them since my early teens, I began by taking some horseback riding lessons at a riding school near where I lived in the UK. This was a traditional lesson barn facility of hard-working lesson horses being passed from one rider to the next—day in, day out. Occasionally, these horses would get to go out on a trail ride or hack off property, but for the most part it was a revolving door of walk, trot, canter lessons. I was taught that in order for my horse to respect me and listen to what I asked, I had to make myself bigger, get after him, and keep insisting until he did as he was told. I was not supposed to let him "win" or "get away with anything."

My response to these tasks and instructions was often one of utter confusion. Inwardly, something didn't sit right for me about what I was being asked to do, and I also didn't really know what was being asked. So I would try and mostly fail.

At a conference a few years later, I got to talking with Gestalt therapist Jim Kepner,[5] author of *Body Process*, a core text in my therapy training. I was in fan-girl heaven, meeting someone who had had such a big influence in my journey of becoming a therapist. We were talking about embodied knowing versus an incongruent way of presenting ourselves bodily, and it struck me that I had never been able to make myself bigger with the horses not only because it was not congruent with who I was in those moments, but because I didn't have the embodied knowledge of what that felt like. It simply wasn't in my repertoire culturally.

From a relational ethics perspective, I wasn't acting from an authentic place of wanting connection but from a place of needing a task to be accomplished. There was no I–Thou relating in what I had been taught to do. I was determined from that point forward to listen to my gut and question the relational ethics of what I was being asked to do with horses rather than sit in silence when things felt incongruent.

While I was living in northern Virginia, I went to a barn to meet a mare that was being offered up for lease. At the time, I was looking for a horse that I could improve my riding skills with, a schoolmaster type that would support me in my attempts at some basic dressage skills. When I arrived at the barn, the owner had already tacked up this mare. The woman explained to me that she was looking to lease out the mare as she didn't have time to exercise her herself due to work commitments. She was also short on time that day, which was why she had already tacked her up ready for me. After watching her ride the horse at walk, trot, canter around the arena for a few minutes, it was my turn to get on and try her out. The owner dismounted and handed me the reins, and I led the mare to the mounting block.

As I stepped up to the block and took my place to mount, the owner walked around the other side of the horse to steady my stirrups. As I swung my leg over the saddle, the mare pinned her ears, turned her head towards her owner, and snapped her teeth at her. No contact was made. In the split second that this happened, I completed my descent into the saddle, and the owner reacted to the mare by punching her three times with a clenched fist on her cheek. The mare, understandably, threw her head up in response, which was met by her owner yanking on the reins under her chin and a loud reprimand of, "Stand still!"

Horrified at what I had just witnessed, I was thankful that the mare had not thrown me off. With shaking hands and legs, I dismounted, gave the mare a gentle stroke to say thank you, and handed the reins to the owner and said, "I've seen enough. Thank you." And began to walk away. The owner, perplexed that I had dismounted, dragged the poor mare out of the arena as she followed me, all the while explaining that she doesn't usually bite like that and that she didn't know what had got into her. Slowly, I turned and faced her. "It's not what she did. It's what you did. I don't want to be part of that way of treating a horse. I don't want to get into a debate with you about this, but I would suggest that you check your horse for soreness rather than beat her up for trying to tell you something. I'm leaving because of you, not her."

In my experience, ethical considerations are rarely that clear cut, particularly within the context of relational ethics. More likely, they will require some soul searching to determine what our course of action will be, presenting us with the opportunity to get clearer about our intentions within those relationships. If we can take this into our relationships with our horses, how might this change the relationship? What would we be challenged into considering? Where do we draw the line for how we interact or what we ask of our equine partners? Each of us will have our own sense of what is acceptable or not. The HERD Institute Codes of Ethics and Professional Practice outline some broad concepts and guidelines, and asking the questions outlined above can help us raise our awareness of what practices may be at odds with our own historical relationships with horses.

While attending my first PhD residential conference several years ago, I met a fellow student who was also an equestrian. After being in classes for a few days, stuck inside the conference facility, we got talking one evening about how much we were missing our various animals and decided instead to bunk off classes the following day to go trail riding at a local facility we'd found online. Another student, who had never been on a horse before, decided to join us, so the three of us slipped out of the building the next morning, feeling excited and mischievous about skipping class.

Upon arrival at the barn, the horses were already tacked up and ready for us. We were assigned our horses, mounted up, and off we went. I was feeling thrilled to be riding a little quarter horse mare that reminded me of Reba. She was sweet but, as expected of many trail horses I'd experienced, not particularly interested in connecting with me. She was there to do her job of plodding along with a stranger on her back. So, I allowed her to go where she wanted, trusting that she would pick her way along the rocky path with confidence, knowing that this was something that she did multiple times a day. I was excited as this trail ride would take us along the beach—something that I had always wanted to experience and definitely on my bucket list—and our guide had promised that we would be allowed to canter along one stretch of it.

The beach ride was every bit as exhilarating as I had imagined, and on our way back up to the facility, my new friends and I chatted animatedly about the experience. As we rode back up the rocky hill, the path extended past the back of the stables. My exhilaration and excitement evaporated as we were met with the sight of the back end of the operation. A herd of around twenty horses stood without shade or water, tacked up and tied to hitching posts. A smaller herd of six miniature horses were hitched to a "live carousel." I asked our guide if they were expecting a big group for a trail ride, thinking (and hoping) that this was why the horses were all standing and waiting. Alas, this was not the case, and I came to realize that this was the standard procedure every day for these horses: stand and wait until needed. The minis attached to the carousel stood there all day, waiting for a child to come along to go round and round.

I felt sick to my stomach. While my friend who was new to the whole horse experience expressed how "cute" she thought the minis looked, I felt horrified at how emaciated they looked. I felt angry at myself for having contributed to their misery by financially supporting an operation that went against my values and wished that I had done more research on the facility before signing up for the trail ride.

Upon returning to the conference, I ran up to my room and immediately called my friend Lis. I was beside myself, and the whole story came out in a muddled tumble of words. To this day, Lis tells me that for the most part all she could make out through my sobbing on the phone was the phrase "those poor ponies" over and over again.

I recognize now that this experience marked a turning point for me in my journey with horses. Where once I always looked for every opportunity to experience the world on horseback, particularly on vacations, eager for the fun and exhilaration of the ride, I now only participate in horseback riding events after researching the ethical practices of a facility. I recognize that all too often my desire to ride in these contexts come at the expense of the horses offered for these purposes. My caution in these situations means that I might be sacrificing a once-in-a-lifetime experience for me, but I'm at peace with that if it means that I'm not contributing to the suffering of another.

Relational Ethics and Mounted Work

The subject of whether or not to engage in mounted work within an equine-facilitated setting is a critical component of our relational ethics. Some models of equine-facilitated work require that sessions be conducted in partnership between a therapist/facilitator and an equine professional, where it is the job of the equine professional to pay attention to the horses' responses during a session. This means that the therapist/facilitator may not be required to be as experienced as the equine professional in watching out for signs of horse welfare and behavior. It also means that the equine professional may not have training in mental health and/or facilitation skills. The HERD Model requires that the practitioner, whether it is an EFL or EFP setting, is dually qualified as both the therapist/facilitator and the equine professional. Indeed, it is our belief that the process necessitates the practitioner to have an in-depth understanding of the equine knowledge and skills found in an equine professional. The practitioner, however, may choose to work with an equine professional if so desired. This is particularly encouraged when incorporating mounted work in order to maintain safety for both horses and humans during a session.

Before we consider incorporating any mounted work, we need to be clear about our scope of practice: When offering mounted work, are we offering traditional horseback riding lessons, therapeutic riding lessons, or something that falls under the banner of equine-facilitated psychotherapy or learning?

As with any other activity we introduce to our clients/participants, we need to be clear about what the aim is for incorporating any mounted work during a session. There are multiple ways of offering a mounted experience within an equine-facilitated setting that can be helpful within an EFL or EFP session. From bareback activities that challenge EFL participants to work as part of a team to support the person that is on the horse, or the embodied process of simply preparing to mount, to encouraging a client/participant to feel the support that a horse is offering while mounted—all are examples of how mounted work might elicit profound learning for clients/participants and bring about meaningful insight. The focus of any mounted experience can highlight embodied themes of balance, movement, and support as well as bring attention to the communication and connection between clients/participants and horses.

Of course, if you are offering a mounted experience, there are many additional factors that must be considered. How will you ensure that your clients/participants are safe while mounted? The HERD Institute adheres to a safety policy where clients/participants must wear a helmet for any mounted experience. You must also ensure that you have enough support staff to attend to each horse when anyone is mounted. If you bring in additional people, whether they are paid equine professionals or volunteers, how will that change the dynamics of what happens within a session? Aside from safety considerations and the logistics of how this might be introduced into a session, how might this impact our relational ethics? In other words, how can we uphold our commitment to work from a compassionate and relational framework with both humans and horses?

Moving into offering a mounted experience shifts the relationship between the client/participant and the horse. For this reason, I usually only introduce mounted work if I am working with an individual or group over multiple sessions. I will also only have one person on horseback at a time. This way I can pay close attention to what is emerging for each person in the moment. The mounted experience can then become part of the relationship-building process, and we can pay attention to how the horse is responding in each moment. Otherwise, the relationship becomes one of I–It, and the horse feels more like a tool.

It's important to remember that the HERD approach is not for the practitioner to interpret for clients/participants what is happening for them in each moment, but for them to attune to their own embodied experiences and allow their meaning to surface. This approach applies both on the ground and in any mounted session. In this way, we can maintain our framework for a phenomenological and relational process with the horses and humans we serve. In order for this to happen ethically and safely, we really need to be familiar with our equine partners.

In my first book,[6] I introduced Elisabeth Crabtree's Human–Equine Relationship Continuum model. This continuum ranges from one end where horses are seen as commodities that we can use as we see fit and treat accordingly, to the other polarity where horses are seen as deities upon whom we should impose zero requirements. In other words, on the one hand, they are tools of the trade, and on the other, they are magical unicorns full of rainbows and glitter. Most of us will fall somewhere in the middle of that continuum, with some of us closer to the magical unicorn than horses as tools. Wherever we sit along that continuum, it will impact on our relational ethics in practice with humans and equines in the work that we do.

Embodying our relational ethics begins with knowing ourselves, our values and beliefs, and having the courage to step up and advocate for those who don't have a voice. It calls for our wholehearted availability for connection, and the desire to form authentic relationships while knowing that this will change us in some way. De Giorgio says: "Personal growth in a relationship with a horse means to become aware of yourself in your interaction with the 'Other,' be able to recognize the 'Other's' perspective, and feel comfortable with what you are experiencing in the interaction."

For me, this is the essence of the I–Thou way of relating that is foundational to the HERD approach. Are you willing to take a risk, to be brave and trust another? Are you prepared to be changed by this moment of connection? Will you allow me to journey with you so that we can experience something together that is unique to us? It is here, too, that Bergum and Dosetter's fourth tenet of environment applies. Expanding the concept of the relational space to include the interconnectedness of all, as well as the situational context, allows us to impact and be impacted by that which is greater than ourselves.

Relational Ethics and I–Thou

How well do you know your horse? Most of us who have spent time with these majestic animals will, at some point in our lives, have fallen in love with one and designated them as our equine best friend. Our relationships with our equine bestie may have been grounded in our experiences of riding, showing, grooming, or simply being with them over time. When we think about them, especially the ones who are no longer with us, we may feel a nostalgic ache and longing for their presence or remember the shared experiences we had. Much like any relationship, connection was built through mutual engagement. I know that when I think about the first horse I ever truly fell in love with, my heart still stops for a beat and my whole body yearns for the smell and feel of him. And yet, I can also honestly say that I didn't really know him. Not in the way that I know my herd now. I loved him, but I didn't know him.

I knew him in relation to human terms. I knew how he would respond to me, his designated human, in various scenarios presented to him from a human perspective. I knew him in relation to what he was like under saddle. I knew what he liked and didn't like in terms of human offerings of treats and carrots. But I didn't know *him*. I didn't really know Rupert, the horse.

While it's not possible for me to transform into a horse in order to fully experience the equine world, it is possible for me to shift my perspective to one that is more equine-centric. This is what Francesco De Giorgio encourages us to do in order to know our equine partners on a deeper level, from a horse perspective. In our way of working within an I–Thou framework, we need to approach both horses and humans with the same intention. De Giorgio says:

> A horse will never be a human and a human will never be a horse. Yet, in the two worlds of perception they each create for themselves, there is an overlap of understanding that we

can learn to recognize and develop together into a shared dialogue that belongs to that particular relationship.

This is precisely what Buber[7] is referring to when he says that there is no "I" without "Thou," and that "I–Thou" is the representation not only of our sense of our selves, but also of being with the Other and how we allow the Other to impact us.

Of course, a horse is a horse, and not human, and humans are not horses. However, relationships are relationships, and how we enter into them, whatever intentions we hold will impact the type of connection that we can have.

Within the context of equine-facilitated work, we are talking here about recognizing the true sentient nature of our equine partners and examining whether you are living into the values you hold. What I love about the zooanthropological approach that De Giorgio supports is that it places the quality of connection at the center of the relationship. He says,

> If we want to share an experience with a horse, to find contact with him and create a dialogue, we must first be able to be in contact with ourselves, as only then can we explore and expand our boundaries and be able to appreciate, understand, and respect the horse's perception of a situation.

By now, I'm imagining that many of you are reading this and asking, "So how do we do this then?" As in any relationship, there is no one-size-fits-all method to this. There is no set activity or workbook that I can give you on how to get to know your equine partners. If I did, it would be the equivalent of me giving you a recipe on how to make friends. Sure, there are some general guidelines based on cultural norms that you might take into account, but in reality whom we connect with and how we make those connections is unique to each relationship. The same applies with our horses.

Whether you spend time in the field with your herd and really get into their mindset through sitting with them, moving with them, sniffing with them, or simply allowing them to be curious with you without an agenda, the important part of the process is in staying curious about what their experience in each moment might be like. The more we do this, the more we can begin to move away from our traditional anthropomorphic way of being with them, so that when we are with our participants, we can truly provide them with a safe space where both horses and humans can bring themselves authentically into the relationship. After all, learning and healing can only be found within a safe relationship.

Part 2

Applications

Chapter 8

Program Designs and Session Plans

In teaching students how to work within an equine-facilitated setting—whether in a mental health capacity, or as educators, coaches, and equine professionals—my belief has always been that regardless of the client population, the priority during any session is that of facilitating relationships through authentic connection. That is, how do we support our clients and participants to bring themselves more fully into the encounter with the horses in each moment and find a way to translate that experience into insights and learning for everyday living?

I've written elsewhere about how to prepare yourself and your horses for the business aspects of this work, so I won't repeat that here. Suffice it to say that it is imperative that you are adequately insured within your scope of practice to operate, and that you are clear about the target market within which you want to practice. Understanding your client population is crucial to what goals you might set for your program, and an initial needs analysis and/or intake assessment must be part of your process.

Whether you are working within the non-profit sector or operating as a private business, you may be called upon to submit proposals for grants or service contract bids. While I have been advocating that equine-facilitated work is not about the activity but, rather, that it's all about relationships, I also understand the need to be able to articulate clearly to prospective clients what it is you will be offering. This may apply to both equine-facilitated learning as well as psychotherapy clients, particularly if you are contracting with a mental health agency, school, or other referring agency. While we are not going to explore the ins and outs of how to write a grant proposal, or discuss the merits of a written mental health treatment plan, what I would like to focus on here is what to do once you have secured the client's commitment to attend your program.

What is the difference between program design and a session plan? How are they formulated? How can I ensure that a program is "successful"?

For mental health practitioners, we may liken this to the difference between a long-term treatment plan and an individual session plan. Depending on the modality of your mental health training, these may or may not be part of your everyday routines. For example, while working with a client with anorexia nervosa, my long-term treatment plan might be for the client to exhibit fewer symptoms of anorexia over a specific time period. My session plans would outline how I might do that from week to week (if that's the modality and frame of reference that I utilize in therapy). I would keep track of this with session notes and progress reviews, potentially within a multi-disciplinary team.

For educators, coaches, and equine professionals, a program design would be the equivalent of your overall curriculum, coaching program, or training routine. The session plan would be your individual lesson plan, coaching, or training focus of the day.

As an educator, I might aim for all my students to be at a particular reading level by the end of the semester. My lesson plans would reflect that overall aim by breaking down what I would teach each week. Similarly, for an equine professional whose training routine for a horse and rider is to aim to compete at an intro-level dressage test, I would break down the pattern that needed to be learned and work on the different components of that each week.

Program Goals, Session Objectives, and Emergent Themes

In a mental health setting, we are often called upon as service providers to document treatment objectives and provide evidence and measurements of our clients' progress. Depending on the context and therapy modality, treatment goals and objectives are either prescribed for our clients, or they might be held within the treatment framework in partnership with our clients. In educational, coaching, or organizational settings, we focus on creating learning objectives that are clear and measurable in order to track both the service user's progress and the service provider's efficacy. As part of the program design process in both settings, it is important to distinguish between program goals, session objectives, and emergent themes.

Program Goals are the areas of exploration that we bring into focus intentionally. These goals may be broad in scope and articulate the type of experience that clients and participants may have as part of the program. These goals often include the identifying need or purpose of the program itself. Program goals are framed with participation language such as "experience," "explore," "discover," etc. For example, goals for an equine-facilitated program might be:

1. Participants will experience working together to improve their communication skills.
2. Participants will explore how breathing exercises can help self-regulation.
3. Participants will discover ways to build resilience through collaborating with others.

Notice that these program goals do not include any specific way in which we might work with the horses in the sessions themselves. These goals may be applied in either EFP or EFL settings and offer the flexibility for practitioners to explore options as they arise during sessions in each moment.

Session Objectives are concrete take-aways for your clients/ participants; they are what clients/participants will have/be able to do as a result of attending the session. Session objectives are framed with observable language such as "demonstrate," "identify," "name," "describe," etc. For those of you who are also PATH International therapeutic riding instructors or educators, you'll be familiar with this from your lesson planning. The point is that session objectives will allow us to track a client/participant's progress. For example, learning objectives in an EFL session might be:

1. Participants will be able to identify three safety guidelines when working with horses.
2. Participants will be able to describe two techniques for self-regulation.

Session objectives for an EFP session might be:

1. Client will be able to identify one or more trigger(s) that lead to feelings of anxiety.
2. Client will be able to describe one way in which they can ask for support from peers.

Notice that these session objectives are more precise, with measurable components. In this way, when we are designing programs with grant proposals in mind, we can begin to articulate the efficacy of our programs. By designing programs in which our session objectives are aligned with the overall program goals, we can demonstrate progression for our clients and participants.

For example, in designing an EFL program for a group of veterans with post-traumatic stress, I might consider one of the program goals to be for participants to support their ability to self-regulate. This would directly lead to a session objective where participants would learn various techniques on how to self-regulate. How we include the horses into that process itself can be flexible and organic.

Emergent Themes are the issues that emerge organically within the session. These may be broad existential themes that correlate with the existential givens of death, freedom, isolation, and meaninglessness; or client population-specific themes that arise as a result of the clients'/participants' interactions with the horses. For example, themes for an equine-facilitated session might be: frustration at being misunderstood by others; indecisiveness in organizational leadership; difficulty in making friends; financial uncertainty during an economic recession; lack of trust and/or sense of belonging; chaos versus control; difficulty in reading social cues; lack of self-confidence; lack of support; or grief and loss.

While all of these themes can be identified through the lens of existential givens, none of them are based in diagnostic or pathologizing language. In other words, for mental health practitioners working in this setting, the theme for a client suffering from depression may not be the depression itself but the existential given of isolation through feeling misunderstood by others or the experience of grief and loss. For the executive coach working with the CEO of an organization, the overall goal of the program might be to foster teamwork for the board of directors, but the theme of the session may be about lack of trust in one another.

Of course, this is just the tip of the iceberg in terms of potential themes that may arise during any session. So how do we design programs with session objectives and goals that can cater to any of the themes that might emerge? What comes first: our understanding of our specific client population and the themes that they are most likely to raise or the session objectives our clients and participants need? It might feel a little chicken and egg at times, and coming up with fresh ideas for sessions can become a challenge. This is why, despite your understanding that philosophically and theoretically that it's not about the activity, the most often asked question is still "What are we going to do with them today?"

Let's Experiment!

Gestalt therapist Joseph Zinker[1] emphasized the importance for therapists to bring themselves into relationships with their clients as a creative agent of change, an improviser, with empathy and compassion. This would be true in the context of equine-facilitated work, be it in a mental health, educational, or coaching setting. As an agent of change and improviser, we can take on the challenge of creating a space for our clients and participants to try out new ways of interacting and connecting with others. We can support them to experiment in a safe space, and allow the novelty of those moments to transform into deeper insights, learning, and healing.

Holding that attitude for our vision of how we want to serve our clients and participants, we need to acknowledge that the process begins before they enter the barn. In our first moments of contact with our potential clients and participants, we are already beginning to feel our way into their world, so that we can design something meaningful with them.

Imagine that you are meeting with the founder and executive director of a non-profit organization that supports survivors of sex trafficking. The organization runs a residential facility for young women, aged 14 to 18, who have experienced trauma and abuse through the sex-trafficking industry. In your discussions with the executive director, you find out that the organization has been offered a grant to fund some equine-facilitated work. While the organization has never offered any equine-facilitated sessions for their residents, the director has heard a great deal of positive feedback about this field and is eager to sign her residents up on a trial basis, with the aim of supporting the young women to build confidence, find healthy relationships, and make safe choices. They would like you to work with a group of six young women, over an eight-week program, where they will come to your facility for two hours per session.

Let's take a look at how understanding the differences between program goals, session objectives, and emergent themes can help us to sketch out a program design.

In this scenario, the executive director has laid out her aims for the participants as confidence building, developing healthy relationships, and making safe choices. In thinking about the program design, an outline of eight-weeks of two-hour sessions for six participants seems fairly straightforward. There is, however, some additional information that I might need before I begin to design the program.

Most important, is the organization looking for you to work within an equine-facilitated psychotherapy or learning capacity? Many organizations will have heard about equine-facilitated work but won't really understand the differences in scopes of practice. Moreover, is the organization expecting this to be a mounted program? If so, is this something that you offer? And if you do, what other considerations need to be examined in terms of the practicalities of providing a mounted session? What about considerations in terms of horse welfare and participant experience, physical ability, mobility, weight, etc.? In other words, what type of experience is the client expecting the participants to have?

Second, in her description of a group of six, it isn't clear whether they will be the same participants each week, or different ones. Does the client want the residents within the facility to take turns so that everyone has the chance to participate at least once? Or are they allowing the residents to sign up voluntarily? If so, how might you ensure participants' suitability for the program? Will some of them come more than once, or are we looking at a "closed" group (i.e., the same participants for the full program, with no newcomers joining the group within those eight weeks).

Once we've established the parameters of the program itself, we can then take a look at the program goals. Based on the aims outlined by the client of building confidence, developing healthy relationships, and making safe choices, we can formulate some clear overall goals for the program.

Examples of EFL Program Goals for This Group Might Be:

1. Participants will create a sense of safety in the group through a process of collaboration.

2. Participants will explore how breathing exercises can help self-regulation.
3. Participants will experience a greater awareness of physical boundaries.

Examples of EFL Session Objectives for This Group Might Be:

1. Participants will be able to identify three safety skills around horses.
2. Participants will be able to describe different ways of maintaining their physical boundaries.
3. Participants will learn how to recognize differences in their respiratory rate.

By taking each of these program goals and translating them into session objectives, it is possible to create an eight-week program. Linking the impact of the program goals with the session objectives allows us to track the efficacy of these interventions.

For example, the program goal of creating a sense of safety in the group through a process of collaboration is aimed at fostering an increase in awareness of the participant's sense of personal safety. Given that a main aim for the client is to encourage the young women to make safe choices, by building this into the program through an experiential process where they are called to make these choices in relation to the horses, we can create an environment where the participants can experiment with a different way of relating.

While these goals and objectives are given as examples for an EFL session, in reality, they can also be applied to an EFP setting. Here, we return to our awareness of scope of practice and the differences in the types of questions we might ask that might allow us to stay within our scope.

But how does this relate to the philosophical and theoretical foundations of the HERD Model? This is where knowledge of the particular client population you are working with is important. Understanding what the experiences and struggles might be and what the participants themselves are hoping for from the experience is also helpful. Thinking about this scenario, the young women in this group may be experiencing a wide range of challenges. Themes that may emerge from the session might be difficulties with:

- Trusting themselves to know what is safe or not
- Recognizing boundaries
- Challenges and/or benefits in staying in the present moment
- What is a safe connection (with horses and humans)
- Identifying issues around choice/freedom
- Authenticity
- Shame and vulnerability

When we are meeting our participants, clients, and horses, we can hold in our awareness the goals and objectives elicited from our initial meeting with the client or referral agency and be mindful of the potential themes that might be prevalent within this client population. We can relate to our clients/participants and horses through a compassionate approach, staying present in the moment, and offering phenomenological descriptions of the process while staying connected and available for an I–Thou interaction. This helps our clients/participants to integrate their experiences into their everyday lives.

Joining the Dots

So how do we support our clients/participants to take the experiential learning from each session back into everyday life? How can we help them join the dots so the insights gained from interacting with the horses will stay with them? How do we track the emergent themes, and link them back to our goals and objectives? If we are working phenomenologically, doesn't this mean that our clients/participants will make meaning of their experiences for themselves and that we won't be able to guide the discussion? What if their experiences don't match the goals and objectives of the session? What if we go off on a tangent during the discussion?

Regardless of whether this is an EFP or EFL session, we can return to our key principles within the HERD models: Here and Now, What and How, I and Thou. If we hold these in our awareness throughout our interactions with our horses and clients/participants, we can begin to see the organic way that everything builds upon these foundations.

Types of Questions

You may have experienced the different ways that equine-facilitated sessions flow (or not) depending on how present you are in the experience and how much you allow (or not) for fluidity in the sessions. At times, it might feel that there is so much going on that it's hard to keep track of what the key insights might be, and how clients/participants might translate those into everyday life.

One way that we can support this process is in the types of questions that we ask. Considering the scenario above and the objectives, goals, and themes that might emerge, we can carve out a few questions that would apply to this client population.

Naturally, one of the challenges that survivors of sexual trafficking face is that of learning to trust themselves and others and learning how to keep themselves safe. Oftentimes, these young women ended up in dangerous situations after being offered a sense of love and attachment by the men who groomed them. They may have felt safe in those relationships until the truth of what was expected of them was revealed. When facilitating a session for this population, we might hold in our awareness that this theme may emerge during a session and consider how that links to our goals and objectives.

For example, in the conversation with the executive director of the organization in this scenario, I already know that one of her aims is to offer the participants the opportunity to experience how to make safe choices. An existential theme of isolation (belonging or not) is likely to arise, and an emergent theme might be whether these young women feel that they can trust themselves to know what is safe or whether it isn't. Since one of the goals for this program is to create a sense of safety in the group through a process of collaboration, we can begin by noticing how the participants respond to the safety protocols given around being with horses. This can be linked directly to the session objectives of being able to identify three safety skills around horses. The real integration and insight, though, is how the process of learning those skills has impacted their own experience of making safe choices.

During the course of the session, the things that I might actively listen for would be their experience and understanding of what "safe" means. I might specifically highlight that process by posing that as a question. I could also pay attention to how they move around the horses and notice if they have taken in the information from our safety briefing and, if not, ask members of the group to remind one another.

The process that is formulated in my mind is as follows:

1. What is the client/participant's experience right now?
2. What meaning is the client/participant making of their experience?
3. How is this relevant in their lives outside of the arena?

So the questions that I ask to link everything together will often be in this order.

1. What are you experiencing right now?
2. What does this mean for you?
3. How might this translate into life outside of the barn?

A more specific example for this client population and scenario—based on the program goals, objectives, and potential emergent themes identified above—might be:

1. What's it like for you to be able to keep safe around the horses?
2. What does it mean for you to know how to stay safe?
3. How might this help you outside of here?

In this way, we can leave space for clients/participants to make meaning from their own experiences and bring attention to the goals, objectives, and themes of each session.

Once again, we need to be mindful of scope of practice here. As an equine-facilitated practitioner within an EFL setting, I may be helped by the questions above to stay within my scope. I do not have consent in that setting to dig into my participants' trauma. My role is to educate, coach, or support them in a way that offers learning. As a mental health practitioner working in this way, I can bring my clinical skills into the mix and intentionally create more openings for the group to experience being vulnerable with one another in a therapeutically safe space.

Chapter 9

Embodied Tracking

Body Process

Historically, society has taken Descartes' view that "I think, therefore, I am" as truth, which suggests that our cognitive functioning is the essence of who we are. The concept of embodiment challenges this perspective and suggests that it is the combination of our mind and body, or our bodymind, that makes up all of who we are. To this end, it means that we experience ourselves through a holistic lens of bodily sensations, feelings, and intuition, as well as our cognitive thoughts. To be fully embodied means that we are grounded in time and space through our awareness of the emotions, sensations, and thoughts in each moment.

Recently, there have been research studies that have identified that what we call our "gut feelings" are our most primary responses to our environment and often occur before our cognitive process kicks in. This also means that by the time we translate our experience into verbal language (which is a cognitive process), we have already experienced it in our body. Language, therefore, is an embodied process, and body language is the source of our primary experience. This links to our philosophical foundations of phenomenology, and Merleau-Ponty's[1] view that we experience the world through our bodily being, so that our experience of our body is the way we perceive the world.

Having lived and worked in different countries over the years, I've had the opportunity to notice and experience differences in cultural body language patterns, both in myself and in others. How we bring ourselves into relationship with others begins with body awareness and language—all the subtle, often unspoken, and culturally situated gestures, movements, and spatial (relational) ways that we inhabit ourselves through our bodies.

In much the same way as other aspects of culture are often out of our awareness, embodied culture can become assimilated to the point of being unconscious. The physical movements and patterns that are part of our culture become a given, and we don't notice how we move, hold ourselves, and use our voices when we are with those who do so similarly. It's only when we are with those who are culturally different from us that our awareness is heightened.

When I first moved to the United States, I experienced a profound shift in my identity. For the first time in my life, I was consistently being referred to as the woman with the British accent as a primary identifying feature, rather than as a Chinese woman. Up until that point, the way that I spoke was not of note to those around me. I was in the cultural majority from that point of view. The way I looked was what separated me out. I also noticed that I needed to adapt certain bodily movements based on muscle memory—looking to the left first rather than to the right for my seat belt when I got into the car and looking to the right first rather than to the left when crossing the street. I even noticed that the speed at which I walked was quicker than most people around me. These are small, subtle movement changes that I have adapted to over the years and took conscious effort. Earlier this year, I returned to England to deliver a training workshop and found to my surprise that I looked the "wrong" way first when crossing the street. Embodied culture in action!

As people who work with horses, we have learned to attune to the body movements of our equine partners. We watch for the energetic, spatial, relational, and intentional movements of each member of the herd, as well as of the herd as a whole. Within an equine-facilitated setting, this is a necessary way of keeping our clients/participants safe. It's also part of our foundational principles of working in a phenomenological way; aside from safety awareness, we are primarily observing rather than interpreting.

Now, imagine if we could translate that same quality of observation and attunement to our clients/participants? What difference would that make in an equine-facilitated session? What additional information might you gain? In the same way as when we are observing the horses, we are not advocating for a prescribed meaning to the body language that you are noticing but simply allowing this information to be part of the bigger picture of what is unfolding in each moment. Traditional body language theories (especially within a management-training environment) like to ascribe specific meanings to certain stances: arms folded equals defensive; hands on hips means confident, etc. While there is some validity in the findings that relate particular postures with shifts in emotional states, we may also be missing the context of that particular individual in that moment. These theories also suggest a more static approach in their analysis of body language: postures rather than movement. As with the horses, we humans are not static creatures, and it's important for us as facilitators to take a holistic view of what is unfolding within the group rather than making assumptions based on one person's posture.

Paying attention to the movements between clients/participants in terms of how they relate to one another also includes body language. Proximity, distance, pace, high or low energy, eye contact, fleeting glances, facial expressions, and gestures are *all* movement based—in the same way as with our horses. I'm sure we all know the statistics related to how and what is communicated: that body language makes up 55% of how we communicate.

While we are not in the business of interpreting what we notice in our horses or our clients/participants so that we can allow them to make meaning of it for themselves, we can turn our attention inward to get to know our own habitual movement patterns. The more we become aware of our own habits and movements, the more we are able to choose our intended communication. Much like raising our awareness of our values and beliefs in order to clarify our relational ethics, learning our movement patterns allows us to be more cognizant of how and why others respond to us in certain ways.

Many years ago, when I first started working in an organizational training environment, my manager observed a workshop I was delivering. Afterwards, he offered me some feedback: "You speak very clearly, and your delivery is good. You project your voice well. What you could work on more is your body positioning when you are presenting. I noticed that every time someone asked a question, you took a step backwards and turned your head away from them towards the projector screen. I don't know if that's because you are feeling uncertain of how to answer the question, but it left me feeling like I didn't want to ask you anything. So I imagine that's what they felt too."

Wow. That was precise feedback. And it was true! I didn't feel like I knew enough to answer questions, even though I knew the material I was presenting. I was experiencing imposter syndrome and felt unsure about stepping in more fully as a voice of knowledge. Being aware of this unconscious stepping away from being questioned gave me pause the next time I presented. Instead of turning away, I intentionally took a breath to ground myself before stepping forward towards those asking questions and noticed how much more engaged the participants were.

Now, at this point, you may be wondering if these techniques go against our attempts to bring ourselves authentically to the process. That they may feel a little contrived. That would be a good question to ask, and if I were to prescribe to you right now ways in which you could move your body to "make" you feel a certain way, or for your clients/participants to feel a certain way towards you, then, yes, I would agree that it would feel inauthentic, contrived, or even bordering on manipulative. So, let's be clear. That's not what I'm suggesting. Instead, my intention is for you to explore this for yourself, so that you can start to notice those moments when you genuinely feel confident, engaged, and connected with others, when you feel you are attuned and in relationship with your clients and participants. In those moments, what do you notice in your body? How are you moving with or towards the other? How do you do that with the horses? Are you able to translate that to how you are with people? Awareness, choice, and practice are the focus.

An Embodied Approach to Tracking Emergent Themes

What is a theme? Within literature, a theme is what the story is about on a deeper level than what is seen on the surface. It's the big meaning, an idea-thread that is woven through the entire story and supports the plot. Often it's moral; love, honor, family, redemption, and revenge are all common underlying themes.

We can think of emergent themes within an equine-facilitated session in a similar way: What is the thread that winds through the participants' stories? This is where our knowledge of the existential givens comes into play. These core themes of death, freedom, isolation, and meaninglessness will show up in various ways during a session. While they may not be articulated in those words, we may be able to elicit the deeper meaning through working phenomenologically with our clients and participants.

While we are tracking the themes and paying attention to our own embodied process, noticing the body language of our clients/participants and horses—all the while staying in the here and now, working phenomenologically, attuning to moments of I–Thou connection, and holding a safe space for all involved—we need to remember that it is impossible to do it all at once! During a session, particularly when working with a group, and/or with more than one horse at a time, there is lot going on in each moment. So how is it possible for us to track it all and stay present at the same time?

Here are a few tips to remember:

1. Know that you will never capture everything in each moment.
2. Breathe and stay grounded yourself. The more present you are, the more available you are for whatever emerges.
3. Stay curious about what the experience is for your clients/participants in each moment.
4. Observe how the horses respond to clients/participants in each moment.
5. Always return to: Here and Now. What and How. I and Thou.

Tracking and Holding Themes
As themes begin to emerge during a session, we can pay attention to how they recur as the session unfolds. Typically, there will be one or two overarching themes that will surface that we can pick up on throughout the session. As clients/participants voice their experiences, we can start to categorize them loosely into broad themes. We can then check out the relevance of these themes with them as we progress through the session. Useful questions in an equine-facilitated session might be:

- How does this resonate with everyone else?
- How does this show up for others in the group?
- How does this relate to what you said earlier about....?
- What else can you tell me about...?
- When this happens, how do you respond at school/work?
- What impact does this have on you all as a group?

Taking into consideration that some of you may be working with neurodivergent populations, particularly if you are working with vulnerable populations, some of the ways in which we connect may need to be adjusted to how these participants interact in relationships. For those who are working with non-verbal participants, or participants with Alzheimer's or dementia, we may need to rely more on body language and kinesthetic feedback. Guiding a participant's hand towards a sensory stimulus and watching for their response or allowing a child to explore the relationship through sniffing or brushing is just as powerful as verbal feedback. It's important to acknowledge that not "one size fits all" when it comes to working with diverse populations.

Viewing the World Through a Different Lens
We all experience the world we live in through our own perspective. The lens with which we view a situation will impact the relationships that can be formed in that moment. Acknowledging that we move through the world within the context of our previous experiences seems like common sense, but we often forget that we all come from different experiences, and therefore, different perspectives. Suspending our judgment and holding an attitude of willingness to meet our clients/participants through their worldview allows us to support them in their healing and learning.

All of our experiences in each moment are processed through the immediacy of the moment. In other words, our attention is always shifting between what is "figure," or most apparent to us, and what is in the background. This continuous process of figure/ground is a core element of Gestalt therapy[2]. When applied within the equine-facilitated session, it allows us to attend to what is most important in each moment. This will also occur for our clients/participants as they move through the process. Paying attention to what is figure/ground for them in the initial stages of meeting them will give us some information on what is important to them. The classic example of the movement between figure/ground can be seen in this picture.

What do you see? An old lady? A young woman? Can you allow your eyes to shift and move between the two? There is no right or wrong, as both perspectives are true. A skilled practitioner is one who is able to shift with their clients/participants between the different perspectives. This is only possible when we are grounded in our own present-moment awareness. A question that I encourage students to continuously ask of themselves is, "What is happening right now?" This encompasses what is occurring in the session for and between clients/participants and the horses, as well as the practitioner's own experience in the moment. Staying with the key principle of Here-and-Now awareness allows us not only to see more clearly what is important for our clients/participants, but also how they are processing their experience. What becomes figural will often emerge as a recurring theme throughout the session.

Chapter 10

All Roads Lead to Rome

Field Theory

The emphasis on awareness of self, other, and environment within the HERD approach to equine-facilitated work is linked to the belief that everything is connected. Whatever figures arise during a session are set against a background and wider context of the clients/participants' lives.

Kurt Lewin,[1] a German psychologist, developed a theory of change called Field Theory in the 1940s, based on the idea that everything is interconnected. He said that in order to understand human behavior, it is important to consider the person within the context in which they exist "as one constellation of interdependent factors." The notion of the "field" refers to all the different aspects of an individual's relationship with their environment that impact on specific behaviors, attitudes, and beliefs at any specific point in time.

Viewing life through this holistic lens may sound obvious to us now, but back in his time Lewis was seen as progressive. His work sparked a multitude of research into child development and psychology and led to debates on the concept of nature versus nurture. Lewin's intention was to deepen our understanding of human behavior through adopting a holistic view of the person in situ of their environment. Within this environment, or field, every element is influenced by and dependent on every other part of the field. Lewin referred to this environment as a person's "life space," which incorporated the physical and social context in which individuals find themselves. In real terms, this includes the places they frequent, events that occur, feelings about places and people, and anything that may influence, condition, or impact them, whether they are aware of it or not.

The interconnectedness in Lewin's field theory is not focused so much on how everything impacts everything else, but more that everything exists in context. As Jane Goodall, legendary primatologist and environmentalist, once said, "You cannot get through a single day without having an impact on the world around you." We all exist as part of an interconnected environment, and every decision we make will have an impact on something or someone.

Since an individual's life space incorporates the totality of what might influence their lives in any given moment, when we apply this to working within a group setting, things can get a little complicated! With each individual's life space bumping up against and/or overlapping another's, it can be difficult to keep track of what is happening for our clients/participants in each moment. So how do we know which figure is more important, and how do we know what thread to follow during a session? This is where a deeper understanding of the phenomenological approach is needed.

Objectivity is an Illusion: Phenomenology Revisited

The phenomenological approach relies on the practitioner to suspend our own interpretations of an experience in order for our clients/participants to make meaning for themselves. In theory, by sticking to the "say what you see" method, we can provide clear descriptions that are not muddied by our own views. Really, though, what does this mean? Both philosophically and theoretically, we have consistently said that the HERD models are based on a foundation of relationships, and that each of us enters into these relationships with our own perspectives of the world. So how do we, or should we, remove ourselves from that relational process? We discussed earlier how important it is for us to remain clear and consistent in philosophy, theory, and practice. How does this fit in with our overall approach?

In reality, any description that we provide is already filtered through our own perception and, therefore, can never truly be "objective." This is fundamental in our understanding of the phenomenological approach. We are not claiming to be scientifically objective. In fact, we are embracing our subjectivity and claiming this as a strength. In this context, subjectivity is not the same as interpretation. We are simply acknowledging the qualitative nature of the process and positioning this method as an embodied and relational endeavor.

While we've talked about building our sense of awareness in terms of self, other, and environment as a way to acknowledge that we exist within our own life space, we also need to move into the space of what we call inter-subjectivity: how what I experience is influenced by what/who is around me, and that I have influence on the other as well. This inter-subjectivity shapes who I am in that moment and influences how I experience that moment. From this perspective, any attempt at objectivity is an illusion.

Now, let's take look at phenomenology in more detail. So far, we have scratched the surface of this field of inquiry by focusing on the skills of providing feedback through phenomenological descriptions. We will now discuss two additional elements of the phenomenological approach: bracketing and horizontalization.

Bracketing
This is the process of putting aside one's own judgments, opinions, and pre-conceived notions of what the experience is for the other. This is why it is so important for practitioners to know their own process and be able to track what is happening for themselves internally. We need to be aware enough of what is our own "stuff" so that we can intentionally set it aside to avoid influencing the outcome or direction of the session we are conducting.

This is where raising our awareness of our implicit biases comes into play. The more blind spots we have, the harder it is for us to bracket out our own assumptions. We need to know what we're putting to one side. I want to emphasize here that bracketing is not the same as dismissing. We are simply paying attention to our own biases, agendas, and judgments that may arise in the interactions with our clients/participants and horses.

Bracketing needs to occur before we offer any feedback through our phenomenological descriptions. This means that we pay attention to what needs to be bracketed, and then we say what we see. This allows our clients/participants to experience their interactions with the horses and bring meaning to those experiences themselves (with the exception of any safety issues, of course).

Horizontalization
This is the process of considering all aspects of what is emerging as equal in potential significance for our clients/participants. In

describing what we see, we accept each aspect of the experience as equally important. So we describe the moment as best we can, as something in that experience will be of value and meaning to our clients/participants. Now, clearly, we are not literally describing *everything*, but it's important to be as detailed as possible in the description we are offering of what is emerging in that moment.

This is where it is helpful to think about zooming in and zooming out, paying attention to not only what is figure to us, or the clients/participants, but also to anything else in the wider environment.

Zooming In/ Zooming Out

Zooming in and zooming out is a process of enhancing our observation skills. If you've ever taken an advanced driving skills course, you'll have experienced an exercise where the driver is asked to say what they see in quick succession, paying attention to both what they observe through their peripheral vision and what is directly in front of them. Without activating the part of our nervous system that responds to hyper-vigilance and potential threats, we can practice this skill by keeping a running commentary of what we are noticing in each moment.

You can practice this when you're out in the field with your horses. Zooming out to the periphery and using all your senses to take in what is happening in the environment around you. What do you hear? What can you smell? What do you feel on your skin? What do you see in the distance? Turn around and look from a different vantage point. What do you notice that is different? During a session, particularly if I'm working with a group, I will intentionally move and place myself in different positions so that I can experience what is emerging from different perspectives. As you experiment with this process, notice what happens in the movement between zooming out and zooming in. What do you notice in your own body? What do you notice in your connections with those around you, humans and horses? Are you able to keep some awareness of the periphery while you are attending to what is directly in front of you?

This process of zooming in and out is particularly important if you are working with a herd at liberty. From a safety point of view, if you are inviting anyone into a space with horses at liberty, you need to be able to keep track of where the horses are and how they are interacting with one another and/or your clients/participants. Even if you have an equine professional to keep an eye on the horses, it's important for you to be able to track the interactions, and movements of the herd. It's also an essential part of being able to pick up on any horse health and welfare issues during a session. As we observe what is unfolding during the session, and provide our phenomenological descriptions, we are holding the space for endless possibilities to emerge.

All the Little Things

A while ago, I ran an EFP session with an individual client who had recently been diagnosed with Attention Deficit/Hyperactivity Disorder (ADHD). Cathy was an only child and had always been told that she was an introverted child who liked to spend time on her own daydreaming. As a 35-year-old adult, she had never had a serious romantic relationship and had difficulty maintaining a steady job. In our initial assessment, she explained that she was struggling with persistent anxiety about getting things wrong in her new job.

During the session, we had entered into the space with the herd, and I had asked her to pay attention to what she was feeling as she observed the horses. I noticed that she had drifted off into her own thoughts while we were standing together in the paddock with my herd of three. The horses were in the shade under some trees at the far end of the paddock away from us, with their heads low. I heard a few birds chirping in the trees behind me, but otherwise it was quiet. In the distance, I heard the sound of a helicopter, gradually increasing in intensity as it approached our area. I felt tension in my body as I wondered how the horses would react to the noise.

I watched as the horses flicked their ears but remained standing still. Cathy was facing the horses but appeared to be lost in thought still. The noise of the helicopter increased, and the horses began to move as one and walked towards us. I felt a sudden movement behind me and noticed the flock of birds that were resting in the trees swoop up and away. Cathy was still standing still, appearing to be lost in her own reverie.

As one of the horses approached, she startled. "Where did you come from?" she exclaimed. She reached out and stroked him on his shoulder, and I noticed Arrow dropping his head and closing his eyes. She continued to stroke him and appeared to retreat back into her own thoughts. The other two horses moved closer behind the gelding.

Choice Points

Paying attention to how the figure/ground shifts during a session allows us to track our client's/participants' process. We might hone in on what is happening between the horses, and thereby make that our figure momentarily, while simultaneously noticing the way the horses are interacting with the client/participant. While it is not our job as practitioners to make meaning of an experience for our clients/participants, it is down to us to follow and track what is figural in the moment.

As always, with so many things going on at once, we need to be able to decide quickly (and often intuitively) what path to take during a session. We call these moments "choice points." In my experience, the saying that "All roads lead to Rome" tends to be accurate here, and for the most part, whichever direction we decide to go we'll end up where our clients/participants need to be. Trusting the process in this way gives us the freedom to go with the flow and flex with our clients/participants.

Back to our example with Cathy: At this point in the session, there were a number of choices available to me:

- Check in with my client as to what she is experiencing in that moment.
- Ask my client what she is noticing between her and the gelding.
- Draw her attention to a potential safety issue with the horses moving closer.
- Stay quiet and continue to observe.
- Provide feedback on any of the details I have observed.

The session continued with me checking in with Cathy as to what she was experiencing in the moment. She responded by saying that she was startled when Arrow approached but was now happy that he was standing there with her. I asked her what else she was noticing about the horses. She looked around and seemed surprised that the others were so close, so I mentioned that it might be good to maintain awareness of how they are interacting with one another as a safety precaution.

As Cathy continued to stroke Arrow, the helicopter hovered directly above us, and all the horses abruptly turned and trotted away to the far corner of the paddock, back towards the shade of the trees. "I wonder why they ran away," she said.

"What do you notice about your surroundings right now?" I asked.

Cathy looked around and appeared to be startled by the presence of the helicopter and asked, "Where did that come from?" I feel like a lot just happened that I wasn't aware of." As she said that, the helicopter began to move away and the noise lessened.

I noticed that the horses had turned and Arrow was walking back towards us, and the birds were circling around and beginning to settle back in the trees. "I see Arrow is walking towards us, and the helicopter is flying away," I offered. "What are you aware of now?"

Cathy looked around her and sighed. She explained that she often experienced this cycle of being in her own world, only to be startled out of it. In attempting to come back into the present moment, she would feel frustrated at herself for "checking out" and feel disoriented. Cathy was aware that this was also frustrating for people around her as she often appeared to be disconnected and disinterested. In reality, when she drifted away, it was often part of her attempt to figure out what she was supposed to be doing next. What I had observed was her processing all the different thoughts that she had about what it was like to be standing in the field with the horses as part of my questions relating to the herd observation, and her inability to organize her thoughts in a coherent way to respond to me.

As Cathy spoke, the birds began to fly out of the trees behind us, and I noticed that they were flying in different directions rather than together as a flock as they had done just moments before. Cathy looked up and around her.

"I see the birds are flying around us in different directions. What do you make of that?" I asked.

"It's interesting that they're scattering like that, don't you think?" she asked. I agreed and mentioned that they had flown in formation when the helicopter was approaching.

Cathy continued, "I feel like that's what happens in my head when I have to concentrate. The more I try and focus, the more scattered I get. The only time that I feel that I'm in formation is when I'm on my own and no one is expecting anything of me."

I shared with her that I noticed how I felt like she was somewhere else while we were observing the horses. I invited her to experiment with an exercise in staying present with awareness and asked her to give me a running commentary of everything that she was experiencing and to let me know when she felt that she might be disconnecting.

Cathy began hesitantly by saying that she could see the horses. I asked her for more detail, and she began to describe them by color and markings. She then moved onto noticing the number of trees, and the color of the fence, and the different shades of green in the foliage around us. She paid attention to sounds, to the birds and the rustling of leaves in the bushes by hidden critters. Slowly, we began to walk around the paddock as she pointed out what she was noticing. The wind picked up a little as we walked, and she said she felt that on her skin. Every now and then, she would pause and let me know that she was starting to drift away. I encouraged her to take a breath before continuing her observations.

As we walked, the horses began to move with us around the paddock. Cathy noticed that Arrow was following her and turned to stroke him once more. I asked her what she was experiencing.

"This guy's been here pretty much the whole time, and I've only just realized that I haven't paid him much attention" she said. "I think I want to stop and just be with him for a while."

This session helped Cathy to notice when she was drifting away and regulate her ability to come back into the present moment. The choice points that emerged throughout the session were all leading to the same place: how to stay or return to the here and now. In increasing her tolerance for being in the present moment, Cathy was able to notice the ebb and flow of connection between her and Arrow.

From a field theory perspective, everything that was in the literal field was of relevance to Cathy in some way. The helicopter, the birds, the horses, and her interactions with Arrow were all part of the mix. In reading this example, what other aspects of the field, or Cathy's life space, might be reflected in the interactions with the horses? What was the existential theme that was most apparent in this example? What was I bracketing in my phenomenological descriptions?

Cathy's experience as an only child who had been told that she enjoyed being on her own had reinforced her tendency to drift away into her own thoughts. What became clearer in our session, and through her interaction with the horses, was how little awareness she had of her surroundings when she drifted away. Through an existential perspective, while this sense of isolation was familiar to her, it also created difficulties in her life. By paying attention to how she was able to connect with Arrow in a more intentional way, Cathy was able to identify those moments when she was tempted to drift away and choose to stay in relationship.

In bracketing my own tendency towards hyper-vigilance to sudden movements and sounds, I was able to stay grounded and present for Cathy. The phenomenological descriptions I provided focused on the here and now, without interpretation of what I thought might be happening for her. While I thought that Cathy looked like she was disengaged, she was in fact trying her best to find words to describe how she was feeling. In bracketing my assumptions, I left space for her to reveal what was happening in her own time.

Through zooming in and out of awareness of what was happening in each moment, I was able to provide feedback to Cathy about the movements of the birds and horses. By noticing what was outside of my immediate figure of interest and holding each element as potentially significant through the process of horizontalization, Cathy was able to indicate what was most significant to her. In this way, the client/participant leads the way while we trust that all roads lead to Rome.

Chapter 11

Activities and Props

In bringing together all the different elements of the HERD approach, we encourage students to think outside the box and allow their creativity to flow. By following your curiosity and engaging your clients/participants with your authentic interest in what is happening in each moment, profound opportunities will emerge. Trusting in the process of the here and now, what and how, and I and Thou, leads us to the magic that so many of us have experienced with our horses, and witnessed for others.

Yes, I understand. While it's not about the activity, it is helpful, particularly for beginning practitioners, to have a session plan in place. This is good practice as it helps to document progress and provide you with a structure for self-reflection and evaluation. Outlining a curriculum or treatment plan is often a good way to secure grants and funding. While designing your program and session plan, you can still allow for some flexibility to give space for figures to emerge from the session rather than utilizing it as an agenda that must be followed.

Thinking Outside the Box

Fresh out of college, I worked in a high-pressure sales environment as a financial recruitment consultant. At the time, I loved my job because it involved helping professionals develop in their careers, looking for opportunities for them, coaching and guiding them in the directions that they aspired towards, and championing them to others. Candidates applying for jobs would become potential clients who would come back and ask me to help them recruit others as they progressed in their careers. Cultivating relationships was the cornerstone of a successful consultant. We worked hard and played even harder, all while looking for the next opportunity to secure a contract. What I learned from my days in recruitment was the importance of attending to relationships, no matter whom I was dealing with. From junior temps to senior directors, every person mattered. I also learned to think outside the box, on my feet, and under pressure.

The multitude of sales training events and conferences I attended helped to hone my skills of working creatively. Interviews involved being asked to role play selling and/or presenting on unfamiliar products. Or inventing new selling points for existing ones: For example, listing in quick succession all the various ways that one might use a plastic ruler other than as a measuring tool trains your brain to think laterally rather than literally. Oh, and in case you're curious, answers included: back scratcher, ice scraper, percussion instrument, adapted catapult (if bendy enough), instrument of torture, blunt knife, flat head screwdriver, paint stirrer, arm extender, and the corners were useful for cleaning under your nails.

These lateral thinking skills have translated well into what I do now. With the addition of training, coaching, and therapy qualifications, as well as the various EFP and EFL certifications I've gained, I believe that every career move I have made has brought me to this point in my life where I need to utilize everything I've learned. From running a business, to sales and marketing, to program and curriculum design, farm management, and being present with those who are seeking support, I have a bank of knowledge and skills to draw on in most situations. That's not to say that I'm done learning; in fact it's quite the opposite. The more I learn, the more I recognize that there are simply not enough hours in the day where I can learn all I want to learn.

This unending curiosity I hold about the world around me is what makes equine-facilitated psychotherapy and learning so rewarding for me. With the support of my horses, I literally get paid to be inquisitive! With each program I design and every session that I facilitate, I learn something new. No two sessions are ever the same, and the unique qualities that clients and participants bring that elicit the mind-blowing responses from the horses give me goosebumps every single time. The connections that are made and the growth that I witness in the presence of horses and humans continue to astound me. Ultimately, as I have been emphasizing throughout this book, it is all about relationships.

Designing Relational Activities

Designing an activity in preparation for a session requires us to be clear about our program goals and objectives. How does the activity you are designing relate to the challenges that your clients/participants are facing? What do you want them to learn or integrate into their lives as a result of the experience? How might the activity enhance, or distract, from the program goals? What equine welfare considerations need to be taken into account?

There are a number of books available that offer examples of set activities, with a list of props required and information on how to facilitate the session. While these can be useful if you feel you have exhausted your own ideas, I find that the activities offered are often complex to follow and regimented in approach. Some activities have been designed without much consideration for how the horses are integrated into the session and feel much more like using horses as tools, while others leave me feeling wary about the lack of attunement to physical safety. I have seen activity books depicting images of people leading horses with the lead rope wrapped around their hands, participants wearing open-toed shoes in the arena with horses, and mounted activities where participants are not wearing appropriate footwear or helmets.

My advice on activity design is to keep it simple. In my experience, the most profound and transformative sessions I have facilitated have involved the fewest of props, if any. The more complicated your activity, the more likely it is that you will become more task focused and at risk of losing sight of the emerging themes and process. It's also much more difficult to keep track of the relational nuances that occur when focusing on an activity. Staying curious and allowing yourself to be creative as the session flows helps us to stay in the present moment.

The biggest mistake that I see students making when designing an activity is creating something that takes too much time to complete. I've seen some really creative ideas that could take a full day to process fully being attempted in the space of a one-hour session. Rushing through an activity to get it done takes away from the relational opportunities in a session and moves us away from the here and now. It's also worth remembering that while grooming a horse may not be a novel experience for you as a seasoned horseperson, for someone who is new to the experience, it can be broken down into smaller steps that take much longer. I once worked with a retired marine in an EFL session where we spent the entire hour brushing out a horse's tail. The horse was at liberty in the paddock and willingly stood still to be brushed the entire time.

Any activity that we introduce needs to consider the horse's well-being. If we are adhering to our values of partnering with our horses and not using them as tools, we need to pay attention to the subtle, and sometimes not so subtle, signs from our horses of what is and is not acceptable to them.

Props

Anything that you already have in the arena can be incorporated into an activity. Grooming, haltering, and leading are simple activities that can promote connection, communication, and boundary setting. Cones, ground poles, and barrels provide simple objects to navigate around, and can be used to represent a multitude of challenges in clients/participants' lives. Hula hoops and giant soccer balls are fun elements to bring into the session. Additionally, pool noodles, basketball hoops, and bean bags can also be utilized in a number of creative ways.

So start with what you already have and brainstorm all the different ways you can use each prop. Here are some suggestions to get you started:

Cones. You most likely already have a number of these in your arena. No matter what size or color, these are useful props as they are easy to move around so you can set up an activity quickly. Ideas for use include:

- Setting up four cones in a square and asking clients/participants to lead horse(s) into the square without a lead rope or touching the horse
- Cones in a square to act as a space where clients/participants must stay within and negotiate space with one another and the horses safely
- Line of cones to weave through with a horse off lead
- Line of cones that represent named obstacles that clients/participants are experiencing
- Spread out a number of cones in the arena/paddock while horses are at liberty. Have clients/participants choose to stand next to a cone and explain why they chose that one. Ask them to move/swap/stay and process what that's like

while noticing how the horses are interacting with them (or not).

Ground Poles. Depending on the type of poles you have, these are usually a little more difficult to maneuver. You may opt to have these set up before the start of your session or invite clients/participants to be part of the set-up process. Poles make excellent props to represent boundaries, bridges, and pathways. They can be used to designate safe or forbidden spaces, or as an obstacle to lead horses over.

Hula Hoops. I love working with hula hoops! They can be used as designated spaces on the ground for people to stand inside or stay out of, or given to clients/participants to hold to represent personal space or boundaries. They can be used as intended as part of a game or competitive challenge. Clients/participants can be challenged with putting a hula hoop around a horse's neck and leading them with the hoop, or as a way to build connection with the horses in a way that necessitates them to pay attention to the horses' reactions as they approach with them.

A word of caution regarding the use of hula hoops. As a safety precaution, it is important to ensure that your hula hoops are cut and re-fitted so that they are able to break away if needed, especially if you are using them to put around the horse's neck.

Giant Soccer/Beach Balls. I'm referring here to the horse-sized arena balls that horses can kick and/or nudge with their heads. These offer opportunities for fun activities like horse soccer or "bowling" tournaments when working with groups, or as part of an obstacle course for clients/participants to engage the horses in play.

With any of these props, allow yourself to experiment with alternative ways to use them. Much like the plastic ruler, thinking laterally about how to incorporate these simple props can help you expand the options you have available to you.

Whatever prop you introduce into the session, it's important that the horses are familiar with it. This seems like an obvious statement, but I have witnessed sessions where the activity itself is based on creating alarm in the horses and watching to see how they self-regulate as an example for clients/participants to learn how to overcome their trauma. This is problematic for a number of reasons, as it indicates a lack of awareness regarding horse safety and welfare, as well as a lack of understanding of trauma-informed care for that particular population.

It's no surprise that practitioners focus so much on activity design. The more practiced we become at letting go of an agenda, the more uncertain we feel about what might emerge within a session. The more uncertain we feel, the more we want to regain control, and the more we want to fall back on set activities. Brené Brown says that there is no creativity without vulnerability. It takes courage to try something new and different.

For me, conducting an equine-facilitated session is an organic process. It is a living, breathing entity that is subject to change dependent on your clients/participants in each moment. There are so many variables that can shift the experience for both the humans and horses present. Each facility has its own rhythm and feel. Each horse we partner with brings themselves into the mix in their own unique way. Each person that walks into the barn looking for support from these majestic creatures will come with their own life space and perspective. None of it is predictable, and the more we try to make it concrete, the more difficult it will be for us to meet the horses and humans as they are, however they are.

Much like cooking, you can plan all your ingredients and follow a recipe, but the process and the result will be something that is unique to you. How you chop your onion will be different to how I chop mine. How much you season your dish will be different to how I season mine. How much you serve and how you present your finished meal will be different to me. You have all the ingredients you need to design an activity, and you have a recipe of what it is that you want to create.

It's not about the activity. It's all about relationships.

Part 3

Case Studies

Chapter 12

Equine-Facilitated Learning Case Studies

The following case studies provide descriptions of actual sessions that I have facilitated. The names and identifying information for all participants have been changed for the purposes of confidentiality. Some of the names of the horses have changed; others appear as themselves. Each of the case studies highlights different aspects of the HERD EFL Model and offers readers an insight into the organic nature of how a session unfolds. Each of the case studies is narrated in a way that allows for flow of reading the story, while also providing notes for a "behind the scenes" glimpse at the thought process behind each choice point. Readers are encouraged to think outside the box for alternative ways to respond in each situation to enhance their own learning.

The first case study takes you through a full cycle of EFL, from initial client meeting, program design, and session planning to facilitating a session.

Remembering our analogy for a recipe, we will begin our journey through the case studies with a reminder of the key ingredients of the HERD approach to equine-facilitated work.

Key Ingredients of the HERD Approach

The HERD approach incorporates the following key elements in an equine-facilitated session:

- Be clear on scope of practice
- Be clear on program design, session plans, goals and objectives
- Have safety protocol in place
- Be aware of existential themes
- Be aware of neurodiversity/cultural considerations

- Include key philosophical foundations
  - o Here & Now
    - Present moment awareness
    - Body process
    - Tracking emergent themes
  - o What & How
    - Phenomenological approach
    - Bracketing, description, horizontalization
    - Figure/round
    - Field theory
    - Zooming in / Zooming Out (All roads lead to Rome)
  - o I & Thou
    - I–Thou Moments
    - I–It is Needed
    - Authenticity
    - Relational Ethics

Case Study 1: Getting to Know You

Background, Needs Analysis, and Preparations

A local elementary school was interested in offering an after-school program to help children who were struggling to make friends at school. They had heard that equine-facilitated learning would be beneficial and invited me to meet with them to discuss a potential program. The initial meeting took place at the school with the school principal and one of the teachers, whose son had participated in some therapeutic riding at the barn that I was working at. They explained that they had a number of students in the third grade that had been diagnosed with autism, and while they were doing well academically, they were struggling with social interactions. At parent–teacher conferences, they had discussed the possibility of offering an EFL after-school program, which parents were willing to pay for, and wanted to get a better idea of what we could offer. The barn that I was partnering with already offered a number of EFL programs, but this would be a new venture for them. I was called in to consult, design, and implement the new program.

During the discussion, we ascertained that the school was hoping for weekly sessions for a pre-selected group of six students aged between 7 to 8 years. They had all been tested as twice-exceptional gifted students, and diagnosed with autism. This meant that while they were strong academically, they struggled with emotional regulation, presenting at times as impulsive, rigid, and/or disorganized. They often missed social cues and often became the source of conflict among their peers. When asked what the educators felt would help these students thrive, their answers pointed towards a program that could help them learn how to make friends through improving their ability to read social cues, communicate more clearly, decrease impulsivity, and increase self-regulation.

Based on the school schedule and facility availability, we offered a pilot for the following semester of weekly one-hour sessions as an eight-week program. The logistics of the program involved the school providing transport to the barn, and parents picking up their children at the end of the session. Liability forms needed to be signed by the school and parents/guardians, and a welcome pack detailing the schedule, suitable clothing and footwear, and emergency contact information would be sent to the parents. Fees were charged in a block for all eight sessions prior to the first session at the barn.

Program Design and Session Plans

The program outline of eight one-hour sessions provided a framework for the sessions. The school had given clear guidelines in terms of their hopes for what the participants would learn through the EFL program. These guidelines became our program goals:

- Improve ability to read social cues
- Improve communication skills
- Decrease impulsivity
- Increase self-regulation

We now needed to translate these into clear learning objectives. With four clear program goals and eight weeks, it made sense to focus on each goal over two weeks. From here, we began to build the session plans (curriculum) for the program, including learning objectives and activities for each week. The program was designed to allow for progression of learning throughout, building on increased familiarity with the horses, fostering connections among participants, and paying attention to the overall program goals. The activities were chosen to provide a framework and focus but were held loosely depending on the needs of the participants each week, and how the horses responded to our interactions with them.

Program Design

Session	Learning Objectives	Activity
1	Participants will learn how to meet and greet a horse. Participants will be able to identify two things that horses like.	Safety protocol Herd observation
2	Participants will be able to identify 2 grooming tools. Participants will learn how to hold a lead rope.	Brushing a horse and introduction to leading
3	Participants will work as a team to accomplish a task. Participants will identify at least one way a horse communicates.	Leading a horse from one cone to the next as a relay race
4	Participants will be able to identify one way that they can ask for help. Participants will learn how to pick a horse's hoof.	Synchronized grooming and picking feet
5	Participants will learn at least one technique to stay focused. Participants will be able to identify two primary needs of horses	5-4-3-2-1 attention game Herd observation of horses grazing
6	Participants will work as a group to overcome a challenge. Participants will practice taking turns while playing a game.	Sharing cones game
7	Participants will learn a breathing technique for self-regulation. Participants will identify two ways in which their behavior impacts others.	Grounding and breathing exercise with horses
8	Participants will learn to give a compliment to another. Participants will identify one way to show gratitude.	Gratitude ceremony with horses

What follows is a description of the session conducted at Week 6. By this point in the program, the participants had become familiar with the routine of coming to the barn and were excited about spending time with the horses. They had learned basic horse safety skills in terms of where to stand in relation to the horses at liberty and were accustomed to starting each session with a reminder of our safety protocol.

In designing the program, I paid attention to the potential existential themes that these participants may be struggling with, namely isolation and freedom. By nature of being neurodivergent, they were keenly aware that they were different from their peers in some way. Their propensity for impulsive behaviors meant that they often felt constrained with what they wanted to do, and had a hard time maintaining boundaries. Throughout the program, we had paid attention to when these themes emerged. This session was designed to explore these themes in more detail.

On this particular day, my co-facilitator, Rebecca, and I greeted the children as they got off the bus as usual outside the barn. We had prepared for the session by placing six different-colored cones in a random pattern in the middle of the arena, and four ground poles in a square at one end of the arena. Our horse partners for the day were Joey and Caroline. Joey was a bay quarter horse, and a retired barrel racer. Caroline was a 20-year-old petite thoroughbred mare, who at her peak was a champion show jumper. The group had met both horses previously, and Caroline had shown a particular interest in one young boy named Derek. While we were observing the horses grazing in the paddock the week before, Caroline had spent the entire session standing next to Derek, occasionally turning her head towards him and tousling his hair with her lips. Derek had been delighted by this, and as he came barreling off the bus immediately asked if we would be spending time with Caroline. After confirming that this would be the case, Derek happily skipped into the barn with the rest of the group.

Gathering around in a circle, we led the group in our safety agreement. In turn, they repeated the phrase "My name is__, and I agree to behave safely, to help keep the group safe." I explained to the group that we would be playing a game with the horses loose in the arena with us, so we would need to pay extra attention to safety and asked them what they thought I meant by that.

"We have to make sure we don't stand behind them."
"We have to stand where they can see us."
"We have to walk slowly and use our soft voices."

Rebecca had already led the horses into the arena, so as we walked towards the gate, I invited the group to stand and watch as she let the horses loose. Joey immediately walked into the middle of the arena and turned a few circles before dropping down on his knees and rolling. The group all giggled at the sight of this. "What's he doing?" asked Megan. "My dog rolls like that when he wants to play," said James, "Miss Veronica, I think Joey wants to play!"

I asked the group how we might play with Joey. "I don't know, I think we have to be friends first," said April. "Okay, so remember when we learned how to meet and greet our horses a few weeks ago? I asked. "How would you like to do that with Joey?"

They looked at one another, recounting how they had learned at the beginning of the program that they needed to approach the horses quietly and offer a "horsey handshake" to allow the horse to sniff their fist before moving closer if they wanted to stroke the horse. "Great job remembering that part," I said.

As this discussion was going on, Rebecca had let Caroline off lead and had rejoined the group. Caroline, in the meantime, had walked around the arena and sniffed at each cone. She then walked to the middle and rolled where Joey had done moments earlier. Joey, who had gotten up and shaken himself off, was now meandering around the arena sniffing at the cones.

> **April:** Miss Veronica, I think that horse wants to play too. It just rolled.
> **James:** That's Caroline, dummy. It's a she.
> **Rebecca:** Remember, we need to speak kindly to our friends, James, and not call people names. You are right, though, that is Caroline. Good job recognizing her.
> **Derek:** That's my friend, Caroline! Look, Miss, I think they're taking turns to play with the cones.
> **Me:** You think so, Derek? What does taking turns mean for you all?

To my amusement, they all started speaking at once. Raising my hand to indicate that I'd like a turn to speak, they all looked at me. "What do we do at school when we have something to say in class?"

I asked. Brad, the quietest child in the group raised his hand. "We do this" he said. "That's right," I replied, "So how about we help each other out with that now? It's a good way to practice taking turns, right?"

With my hand raised, I explained that we would be entering into the arena with the horses and taking turns to go and say hello to each of them. I invited them to go and pick a cone that they wanted to stand next to, one cone per person, and when they were ready to raise their hand. We watched as they walked around the arena. A couple of them went directly to a specific cone, and the others meandered around a bit before deciding on the one they wanted. April and James approached one of the cones at the same time. I waited to see how they would navigate this moment with each other. April paused for a beat before looking around for a free cone. Joey was standing next to the only one available.

> **Me:** What's happening right now, April?
> **April:** I wanted this cone, but James is there and there isn't another one free. Well, there is, but Joey's there, and I don't know if that counts.
> **Me:** It counts, but I like that you checked. What would it be like for you to stand next to Joey at that cone?
> **April:** Okay. I can share it with him

At that, the rest of the group started chiming in with protests of wanting to share their cone with the horses. The original plan for the activity was to have each child stand at a cone and take turns to go and greet the horses. We were then going to introduce a "musical chairs" type game into the mix by playing some music, then stopping it and asking the participants to stand at a cone. Each time we played the music, we would remove one cone, and the person left standing without a cone would have to go to the island (square made with ground poles) and wait to be rescued by the horses. If they could get the horses' attention and either one of the horses came over to the island close enough to be touched, the person would be rescued.

Now, the situation was presenting a new possibility. We had the choice of continuing with our planned activity or following the lead of the group, whose focus was a desire to share their cones with the horses. I briefly considered how we might adapt the original game and decided to go with the flow of the figure of learning to share what was emerging from the group. Looking over at Rebecca, I indicated that we would be adapting the game.

I raised my hand. "Okay. So who would like to share their cone with Joey?" I asked. Four little hands went up. "Who would like to share their cone with Caroline?" Derek and James raised their hands. I asked them to consider whether this was a fair request of the horses with four people wanting to be with Joey and two with Caroline. I wanted to ensure that Joey would not feel overwhelmed by the number of people around him. They decided that it should be three people per horse. I asked them how they might decide which of the four who had wanted to be with Joey would switch to Caroline. After some discussion, they decided that the fairest way was to split the groups as girls and boys. April, Megan, and Jessica would go with Joey, and Derek, James, and Brad would be with Caroline.

As they discussed this, Joey continued to stand at the cone with April. She had occasionally reached across and stroked Joey while the group was discussing what to do. Caroline, in the meantime, had approached the ground poles and was standing in the middle of the square, with her head low, and eyes closed. The sun was shining through the open doors of the arena directly into the square.

I invited them to stand together in their two groups and look around. "Before we split up into our groups with the horses, take a look around and tell me what you notice."

Jessica: Caroline is sunbathing.
James: Joey is sleepy.
Megan: It's really quiet in here.
Brad: The cones aren't in a square. They're just all over the place.

I asked if there was anything they'd like to change in the arena. The boys wanted to turn the cones into a square. The girls wanted to stand in the sun. I was aware that we now had additional choices: Caroline was in the sun, but Joey was not. The group had decided that the girls would be with Joey, but they also wanted to be in the sun. Do we facilitate Joey moving to the sun and disturb him, or focus on increasing tolerance for things not being perfect and appreciating some of what you want? For me, this was an easy choice to honor the horse and turn this into a teachable moment.

I turned my attention back to the group to point out our choices. I invited the boys to pick four cones to make a square around Joey, and asked the girls to approve the set-up once they were done. Happy with what they had constructed together, we were now able to split the group to spend some time with each horse.

Returning to our original idea of introducing music, I explained that each person would take turns to pet the horses while the music was playing. When the music stopped, they would step back and let the next person have their turn. The horses were allowed to leave the square, but they were not. If the horse left the square, they would need to find a way to get the horse to come back. The aim of the game was to figure out a way to pet the horses so that they liked it so much that they would stay.

Turning the music on, I encouraged those waiting their turn to notice how the horses were responding to being touched. Joey stretched his neck up while April scratched under his chin. Caroline slowly yawned and arched her back as Brad stroked her gently on her side. I stopped the music and the next person stepped up in each group for their turn. Caroline turned and tousled Derek's head as he approached. Joey took a few steps forward and almost stepped outside the square of cones but stopped and stretched down to scratch his nose on his knee. Megan took this as a sign that this was where he wanted scratching and bent down to scratch his knee. I stopped the music.

With one more person from each group to have their turn, I was about to start the music up again when a car alarm went off in the background. The horses lifted up their heads in unison and walked out of their respective squares towards the gate to a chorus of disappointed cries from the group. We had 15 minutes remaining before the end of the session.

I asked them what it was like that not everyone had had a chance to pet the horses. "It's not fair. I want to help get Caroline back so James can have his turn," said Derek. "Same here for Jessica," said April. I reiterated the rules of the game to the group and let them know that we had about 10 minutes left.

Each group started calling the name of their horse. The horses turned their heads towards the groups but remained by the gate. The children clucked at them, they whistled, they made kissing noises, all at the same time. After a minute of this cacophony, I raised my hand and they stopped. "How's it going?" I asked with a smile.

> "They're looking at us but not moving!"
> "They look confused."

"They don't want to play anymore."

"How can we help them understand what we're asking? I hear you clucking and kissing and whistling all at the same time. I see them looking at you." I said. They considered this for a moment. "Maybe if we all did the same thing at the same time?" ventured Jessica. "Maybe we could clap together?"

The group agreed that this was a good idea and started clapping slowly and rhythmically. I watched the horses orient their bodies towards the two groups and smiled as I saw James pointing at Derek's head as an incentive for Caroline. As they continued to clap, they got faster and louder. The horses began to move towards them, and the clapping turned into cheers. Caroline stepped over one ground pole, leaving the rest of her hind end outside the square. James stepped up and gave her a hug. Joey walked back across the arena to the square of cones and paused on the outside. Jessica reached out and stroked his shoulder. He turned and took one more step towards her placing one foot inside the square. It was good enough. Rebecca and I cheered.

We invited the groups to say thank you to the horses before we wrapped up the session. Checking in with each of them, I asked what they were taking away from their experience. "It's fun to do things together," said April. "I liked helping get Joey back in the square" said Megan. "I can take turns and be patient" said Derek.

This case study highlights the way that a program activity can be adapted during a session to fit what is emerging in the moment. By focusing on the here and now, phenomenological descriptions, and I–Thou interactions with the horses, we were able to facilitate an experience that was meaningful for the participants in such a way that tied in with the program goals and learning objectives. The participants left with a sense of accomplishment at being able to support one another, which alleviated their feelings of isolation, increased their capacity for taking turns, and reduced the likelihood of impulsive behaviors in the moment. The horses were allowed to move with freedom and choice within a framework of safe practice, which made their willingness to engage much more meaningful.

Case Study 2: Creating Space

Anna was referred to me through a colleague in Spain. A British woman in her early 50s, Anna had taken early retirement after working as a high school teacher for 35 years. She had recently relocated to Tenerife, in the Canary Islands off the coast of West Africa and was interested in attending an individual three-day retreat with me in Florida. Through our initial email and telephone contact, Anna had indicated that she was interested in creating a nature retreat to work with mothers and daughters looking to improve their relationships. While her vision was not equine-facilitated focused, she wanted to experience an EFL retreat to help her gain clarity for her program.

Anna arrived at my Orlando-based facility in early January. It's a beautiful time of year for being outdoors in Florida. The temperature is comfortable and usually dry, giving us a reprieve from the hot, humid summer months. For a three-day retreat, the program format is a mixture of spending time actively engaged with the horses, observations at a distance, and room-based coaching sessions to further enhance the experience with horses. These individual retreats are customized to the needs of the participant and free flowing in design. While I hold an awareness of the goals that participants come with, the interactions with the horses are organic, and activities will often arise in the moment and are co-created with the participant.

This particular session occurred about halfway through the retreat. We had spent time exploring her motivation for creating her program, created a mind-map of her business strategy, and spent time with the horses in herd observation and grooming. Anna had realized through the process that she was anxious about launching the business for fear of what her family might think. As a divorced mother of four, she had experienced strained relationships with her only daughter. While this formed part of her motivation to support others through difficult relationships with their daughters, she wondered if she was qualified enough. Her daughter, who was a licensed mental health practitioner, had commented in the past that she didn't think Anna had the skills to offer the kind of retreat she was describing because she isn't a therapist. This had knocked Anna's confidence, and she wanted to know how she could do this work without being outside of her scope of practice. Anna felt that her background as a high school teacher meant that she could offer educational and experiential programs in her area without overstepping her bounds.

For this session, my plan was to lead Anna through a visualization exercise so that she could get a clear sense of what it might feel like to step into this work. We had already developed a routine of starting each session outside, sitting on some folding chairs facing the paddock where the horses were grazing. As Anna lowered herself into her chair, she let out a big sigh, then shook her head, leaned forward, and put on a big smile. I commented on what I'd observed, and she leaned back into her chair and sighed again. She was putting on a smile because she knew that this was going to be a tough session but felt determined to soldier on.

> **Me:** What does soldiering on look like to you?
> **Anna:** To get it done, even if I don't want to.
> **Me:** What choices do you have around that?
> **Anna:** Well, it's all up to me, but it's just hard to put myself out there knowing that people will make judgments about what I'm doing.
> **Me:** What judgments are you making?
> **Anna** (laughing): That the whole thing will be a flop and no one will come! Although, I suppose that's more of a fear than a judgment.

As she said this, I noticed my two mares walking in our direction. Cheyenne walked up and stretched her neck over the fence and sniffed in our direction. Reba stood directly behind her.

> **Me:** I see that Cheyenne and Reba have come over. What's that like for you?
> **Anna:** Haha! Maybe they're telling me that people *will* come, and it doesn't need to be a big show-and-tell. We just sat here, and they came over. Maybe it can be that simple.

I asked Anna to tell me more about her vision in terms of the space that she wanted to create. She described her property in Tenerife, a 30-acre farm in the mountains with incredible views. An avid gardener, she had already cultivated an organic vegetable garden with the aim of offering farm-to-table baskets for her clients. Aside from the farmhouse that was Anna's home, the property had a separate three-bedroom guesthouse. It was rustic but had a fully functioning kitchen and bathroom. Her plans were to upgrade the guesthouse with cozy furnishings and create a patio area for guests to sit outside to enjoy the views overlooking the valley below. The land itself provided ample options for bike riding, hiking, and walking, with several trails already cut out and more planned. There was a large stream that ran through the property that provided options for fishing or swimming. The woods on the property meant that guests could learn to forage for edible plants. A big campfire area could be set up in the woods for evening sessions.

As she talked, Anna became more animated. Her eyes were bright and her hands gestured in the shapes that she described. The horses had stayed close by, grazing in the paddock, moving slowly and flicking their tails. The more Anna described her property, the more restless I began to feel. I checked in with her to ask what she was noticing. "I feel like I want to walk around," she said. I invited her to stand up to get a feel for where she might like to walk. "I don't think I want to be inside the paddock. That feels too confined. I want to be out in the open. Maybe we can walk down the driveway and back?" I nodded and motioned for her to lead the way.

I have a long driveway that has a loop at the top end near the barn. We walked to the end of the driveway and turned back towards the barn. In the distance, I could see the mares had moved to the corner of the paddock and were facing us, heads up, ears forward, and watching. I pointed this out to Anna, who smiled and said that she thought they were wondering if we were leaving. As we walked back towards the barn, we took the loop on the far side away from the paddock and walked past my chicken pen. The chickens were squawking loudly and ran from one end of the pen to the other as we walked by. Meanwhile, we were out of sight of the mares, who had started whinnying loudly.

> **Me:** What are you noticing now?
> **Anna:** Everyone seems to have an opinion! It's like I can't go anywhere without someone noticing. The horses can't see us and want our attention. The chickens see us and want our attention.
> **Me:** What does that mean for you?
> **Anna:** Like it doesn't matter what I do, someone will have an opinion, so I may as well do what I want to do.

Anna paused, slowed her steps, and turned to me, and grinned. "I'm not launching this because I have to. I'm launching this because I want to." I asked her what that was like to say out loud. "Motivating. Exciting. I really want to figure this out and make it work now."

We walked back towards our chairs. The horses were waiting at the gate next to each other. I asked Anna what would help her to really visualize her program. "I'm not sure. I think I need to be in it. To be there and feel it around me." I wondered if it would be possible to create that for her, perhaps mapping out the layout of the property in the arena, so that she could stand in it and feel it around her. "Yes! Let's try that," she said.

I invited Anna to take a look at all the props I had available in the arena and to create from them (or anything else that she found lying around) a topographical map of her property. Grabbing cones and ground poles, barrels and hula hoops, Anna set about positioning them around the arena.

My arena opens out into the back paddock where the horses were grazing. So I kept an eye on their movements while Anna was busying herself with setting up her space. Cheyenne and Reba watched from a distance for a while, then gradually made their way towards the arena gate. They stood at the fence looking into the arena. My gelding, Arrow, continued grazing at the far corner of the paddock, away from us.

> **Me:** I see Cheyenne and Reba standing at the fence.
> **Anna:** I know! I think they're a bit confused as to what's going on. It's a bit of a mess in here right now.
> **Me:** I notice that Arrow is staying on the other side of the paddock. What do you make of that?
> **Anna:** Hmm...that's interesting. Maybe he's picking up on the fact that I'm creating something for women only. Maybe that's why Cheyenne and Reba are so interested.

Anna stopped her bustling in the arena and came over to the fence. "If you two were mother and daughter, what would you be interested in?" she asked. Walking around so that she was positioned on the same side of the fence as the mares, Anna reached up to stroke Reba on her shoulder. "Maybe you can show me where things need to be. Let's go in the arena."

Anna walked with purpose back through the arena gate, clucking at the horse as she went. Reba slowly followed her in, with Cheyenne close behind her. Once inside the gate, the mares looked around at all the props scattered around the arena. While they are used to these items, it's unusual for all of it to be in the arena at the same time. Cheyenne walked over to a cluster of cones that Anna had left near the middle of the arena and sniffed at them. She pawed at the sand next to the cones, knocking a couple of them over. She circled around and came at them from a different angle and pawed at the sand again. Stretching her neck out, she deftly picked up one of the cones with her teeth and threw it to one side. One. Two. Three cones were tossed away, creating more space in front of her. Slowly, she lowered herself to the ground and rolled. Anna laughed as she watched Cheyenne.

> **Anna:** I guess she wanted to create some space for herself.
> **Me:** How does that resonate for you?
> **Anna:** Well, maybe I need to start with small step, rather than try to do it all at once. I can create something and build on it instead of waiting until all the pieces are in place.
> **Me:** What might that look like here?

I gestured to the props lying around the arena. Anna put her hands on her hips and surveyed the scene. "I suppose I could start by getting rid of the cones. I was going to use this to represent the new trails I have planned through the property. But there are existing trails that I can use for now."

She proceeded to remove the cones and put them to the side of the arena. Next, she picked up the ground poles and positioned them at one end of the arena in a square, explaining as she went that they represented the guesthouse and patio area on the property. She took one of the hula hoops and positioned it at the other end of the arena, designating it to be the campfire, and moved the two small barrels next to each other in the middle to represent the woods.

Reba positioned herself next to the barrels and stood with her head low and eyes half closed, while Cheyenne continued lying on the ground, legs stretched flat out. "I think they're taking a nap. What a great idea. That was a lot of hard work, wasn't it, girls?" said Anna. "That's another thing that worries me about my plan. I'm doing this all on my own. It's a lot to take on."

> **Me:** What help might you need?
> **Anna:** I'm not sure right now. But I know that I'll need to take care of my energy levels; otherwise I'll end up getting overwhelmed and taking on too much.
> **Me:** What's your energy level right now?

Anna: That was hard work moving all that stuff around. Maybe we can sit down for a while.

Leaving the horses in the arena, we retrieved our folding chairs from outside the paddock. When we returned, the horses hadn't moved an inch. Anna chose to position her chair inside the ground poles that represented the guesthouse, and I joined her with mine. Looking out across the arena at the props and the horses napping in the sunshine, I was aware of how quiet it was. Anna took a deep breath and closed her eyes, tilting her face up towards the sun. Slowly she opened her eyes and looked around once more.

Anna: I've been so worried about what others might think of what I want to do, and now I realize that it doesn't matter. It's what I'm passionate about. I can feel what it might be like for my clients to come and unwind, enjoy the property, and reconnect with each other. Look at the horses! They're just chilling out together in the space I've created. That's what I want for my clients!

As she said this, Reba walked towards us. Standing next to Anna's chair, she dropped her head to her shoulder and exhaled. Anna reached up and hooked her arm under Reba's neck and stroked her. I gave space for them to be together for a few minutes before asking her what she was taking from this experience. "I need to trust my gut, give myself time, and not try to do everything all at once. I'm realizing that if I focus so much on getting things done, I'll miss out on connections like this with people around me." Anna looked up at Reba. "If I hadn't seen the horses relaxing, I wouldn't have thought to sit down, and if I hadn't sat down, this wouldn't have happened."

This case study highlights the importance of staying with the here and now, what and how, and I–Thou throughout a session. The existential themes that emerged for Anna were centered on freedom and meaninglessness, realizing that choices were available and finding purpose and meaning in what she was preparing to offer the world. In working with Anna, I paid attention to the wider context of her life space in terms of her habitual pattern of soldiering on and her fear of judgments from others.

In zooming in and out of awareness between self, other, and environment, I called attention to the figure that was emerging, as well as the background. The fact that Arrow had chosen not to join us was as significant as the fact that Cheyenne and Reba had. The quietness of our surroundings in the arena added to the peaceful quality of what Anna was hoping to provide for her clients. The moments of pause to allow for connection and meaning-making brought a more profound awareness for Anna of what she was hoping to create in her space back home. Allowing the horses the freedom to wander in and out gave Anna a sense of freedom and increased her awareness of the choices that she could make in each moment. Holding space for the possibilities of Anna's creative expression of what she was experiencing, rather than offering a set activity for her to explore, resulted in her gaining a deeper sense of integration to her learning.

Case Study 3: Signals

I was recently asked to facilitate an EFL session with a group of senior executives from a US-based global technical engineering firm. The company has offices worldwide, with a multi-million-dollar portfolio. Due to company-wide restructuring, the C-suite directors wanted to experience a team-building event with their first-line reports that would kick start the new financial quarter, and allow them to get out of the office and do something different. From my conversations with the human resources director, I was aware that the chief executive, chief financial officer, and the chief operations officer would all be in attendance. They wanted to utilize the half-day event to include a team strategy meeting that would reflect the learning from their session with the horses. There were 24 people in total coming out to the barn, and I needed to design a program for the event to suit their needs, in collaboration with the facility I was partnering with.

With so many people, my first thought was whether it would be safe to have everyone in the arena at the same time. They wanted a team event, so it was assumed that they wouldn't be split up into separate sessions. The timing of the event meant that the facility was limited in who I could bring in as equine support, so essentially I needed to manage all of them, plus horses, with only two other people. Knowing the horses at this facility, I knew that we couldn't expose them to large groups of people at liberty. While they were accustomed to working with groups, it had never been for so many all at once. We needed to come up with something that was interactive enough for everyone to take part in while attending to issues of safety and horse welfare.

After additional discussions with Katie, the human resources director, it became apparent that because of the global nature of the company, many of the participants would be meeting face to face for the first time at this event. They were flying from across the United States, United Kingdom, Europe, and China. There would be a number of participants whose first language was not English and who were not fluent, although they all spoke and understood English well. This added to the mix the consideration for cultural differences and an awareness of how things may be lost in translation. Speaking with the CEO prior to the event gave confirmation that this is often the case, and that improving communication was a priority.

From this information, we designed a four-hour event to include a working lunch for the team's strategy meeting. Our goal was to provide an experiential learning opportunity with the horses to spark discussions of next steps in their strategy meeting. In particular, we wanted to focus on the concept of attunement and awareness—how to read the more subtle communication cues from those around us. My interactions with the CEO had given me the sense that the organizational culture was one of constant reaching for more, and once one goal was achieved another appeared immediately on the horizon. As with many successful individuals, the CEO didn't see anything wrong with expecting the same drive he had for perfection and continuous improvement from everyone on the team. In contrast, the human resources director had commented that the constant pressure to deliver without an acknowledgment of achievement was taking its toll.

Our program goals were clear. The session objectives were set as follows:

1. Participants will be able to identify moments when they need to pause.
2. Participants will identify moments when they need to ask for clarification.

Our session plan involved a staged process of introduction, starting with facility orientation and an introduction from the human resources director, followed by introducing myself, and my co-facilitators, Julie and Robin, who were on hand as my equine support staff. We would prepare the outdoor arena by setting up a

50-foot-round pen in the middle, and would be partnering with three horses, Misty, Jack, and Star.

In an effort to maintain safety and keep the group together, we wanted to have the humans inside the round pen while the horses were at liberty around them. We thought it would be interesting to see what this would bring up in the group in terms of existential themes of freedom and isolation. Given that the company had recently undergone a major restructure, tensions were still high with regard to job security, so we also wanted them to pay attention to the horses without having to worry about safety—existentially and literally.

Our plan was to have the participants observe the horses for a few minutes, discuss what came up from that, and then transition into a more hands-on meet and greet of the herd. We planned to bring several blindfolds along to use for the purpose of asking for three volunteers to be guided while blindfolded by a colleague and interact with one of the horses. Three pairs, three blindfolds, three horses. The rest of the group was to remain in the round pen to observe the interactions. We wanted to provide as much hands-on time with the horses as possible while being mindful of the horses' tolerance to being surrounded by people.

We also planned to place three lines of four cones on either end of the arena, and one in the middle outside the round pen for the purpose of teaching the participants to lead the horses through the cones, culminating in a synchronized leading exercise. By splitting the 24 people into three groups of eight and having four people at each end of the cones, they would lead the horses in their groups of four (two people on each side of the horse), hand the horse over to the next group, and make their way back through the cones like a relay. The aim would be to lead the horses, weaving through the cones, in time with each other so that all three teams would finish at the same time (see diagram below). That was the plan.

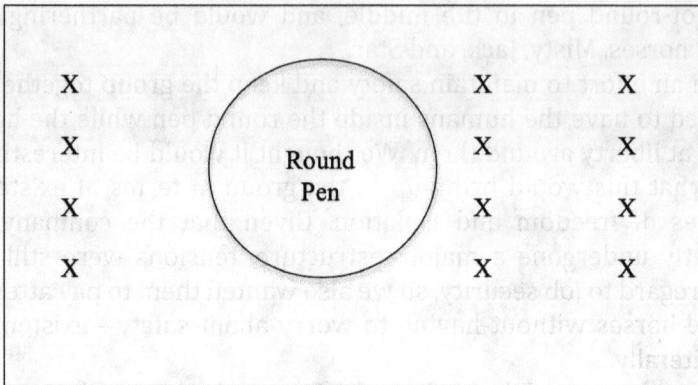

On the morning of the event, I arrived early to get everything set up. Julie and Robin had already arrived to make sure that the horses we were working with were groomed and cleared to work, with no health issues. As the participants began to arrive, we directed them into the classroom and double checked that all liability waivers had been signed, and that everyone had come with suitable clothing and footwear. There was a feeling of great anticipation for the event as, unbeknownst to us, the CEO had told everyone that they were coming to the barn to ride. We had made it clear to him during our initial meetings that this would not be a mounted activity but he had taken it upon himself to tell the group that they would be riding as a joke. So right from the beginning, the expectations of the day had to be managed.

We began with our introductions, and Mike, the CEO, spoke about his vision for the day as "something that would provide the team with food for thought as uncertainties emerge over the next few weeks and months," and how important it would be for everyone to align with company values. He emphasized that he needed to have "all hands on deck to push through this wave of uncertainty, as it's no time for resting."

I looked at Katie, the human resources director, who was my main contact for the event, and she looked shocked. Catching my eye, she shrugged her shoulders. The scene that Mike was setting was 180 degrees from what we had discussed and what we had in mind as our session objectives. Katie stepped in to continue setting the scene for the day, talking about timings and logistics before handing proceedings over to me. At this point, I was still feeling a little blindsided and was curious whether this was something that happened a lot with Mike and his team. I felt tension in the room.

I started by introducing myself and the rest of the team and addressing a few housekeeping points. I was aware that a few people on the team had not met in person before, so we went around the room for everyone to introduce themselves, and I asked them to say something about what they were hoping for from the day, and whether they had any horse experience. Several people mentioned vacation trail rides, but for the most part, the group was unfamiliar with being around horses.

The common themes from their expectations of the day were the need to keep an open mind, and to expect the unexpected. Clearly, this was part of the team's culture, and Mike's leadership style included keeping people on their toes. I wanted to set the scene before we went out to meet the horses. My internal dilemma was how to address the inconsistencies of what Katie had shared with me in terms of what the team needed—i.e., clearer communication and attunement to others and to feel safe enough to pause and ask for support—with what Mike had just outlined for the team. It wasn't up to me to call him out in front of his team, and this event wasn't to challenge his leadership skills, or style. I needed to find a balance.

> **Me:** I hear quite a few of you mentioning the need to expect the unexpected and listening to Mike's introduction to the day I hear that uncertainty is the only thing that is certain. That, and a lot of hard work, right? I'm also aware that you were all told before coming here that you would be riding the horses today, only to find out that's not the case. So, there are two types of uncertainty here: one is not knowing at all what's coming next, and the other is when you're focused on one goal and the goal posts shift. So, I'm curious about how you all deal with that. Our job is to help you figure some of that out and look at what we can do differently as a team to support each other in those moments. That's what we'll be focusing on today.

Katie looked over and smiled. Mike and the rest of the team nodded. We were good to go. With that, we mobilized and headed outside. While Julie and Robin went to fetch the horses, I led the team through a brief grounding and awareness exercise. I wanted them to begin to bring themselves into the present moment. Given that the team spent so much of their time rushing from one task to another and travelling from one place to the next, I wanted to deliberately slow down the pace. It also allowed me to keep grounded myself.

I then led the team through our safety protocol. I'd printed out copies of the safety agreement and handed them out to everyone so that we could all read it out loud together. "My name is____, and I agree to take responsibility for my own safety, in order to contribute to the safety of the group." I briefly talked about safety in terms of horse blind spots, watching where your feet are in relation to the horse, and how to greet them with a horsey handshake. With so many people in the group, I wanted to ensure that the horses didn't become overwhelmed by people touching their faces, so I encouraged them to pet the horses on their neck or shoulders.

As Julie and Robin entered the arena with the horses, I invited the participants to step into the round pen. I gave them instructions on our herd observation exercise, encouraging them to pay attention to stories they might be telling themselves about what they were observing in silence. As they entered the round pen, they were in good humor and joking with one another about being caged, and someone commented on it being like a UFC boxing octagon.

Misty, Jack, and Star were let loose in the arena. Jack, an inquisitive Paint gelding, immediately trotted up to the round pen. Taking his time, he slowly walked all the way around in one direction, and then turned and walked all the way back the other way, all without stopping. Star, a petite bay quarter horse mare, kept her distance from the round pen, walked to one corner of the arena, and stood facing outwards and away from the group. Misty, a big grey Percheron mare, started walking towards the round pen and stopped by the set of cones in the middle of the arena. She sniffed each cone, turned at the end of the line, and proceeded to walk back, kicking each cone as she went, knocking them over and/or out of place. Jack looked over at Misty for a moment, tilted his head, flicked his ears back and forth, and blew out. He then continued his journey around the round pen, but this time, stopped after every couple of steps to tilt his head sideways and stick his muzzle through the railing. I noticed a few people step forward to scratch him on his muzzle, and a few people back up as he approached. "What's happening for you all right now?" I asked.

"That one doesn't seem to want to be involved. She's all the way over there by herself."

"I don't like being in here while they're out there."

"I like it in here. It feels safer."

"I loved it when this one started sticking his head in to get closer to us."

"I thought it was interesting how he took his time before deciding what to do with us."

"I liked how that one trampled all over the cones, and then got told off."

"I think this one's the boss. That's why he's doing the rounds and checking us out."

The themes that were beginning to emerge were based on isolation, connection, safety, freedom, expectations, and time. I was curious as to where this would lead, so encouraged them to spend a few more minutes observing and to notice what might change after hearing what others were experiencing.

Jack wandered over towards the fence next to Star. He stood quietly next to her for a few moments. Suddenly, he turned with his ears pinned back and snaked his head at her. Star backed away from Jack, stopped a few feet away, and shook her full body before turning her back and walking to the opposite corner of the arena. Checking in with the group, I asked them what they made of that interaction.

"Jack's definitely the boss!"

"That kinda came out of nowhere, though. They were standing together peacefully, and then he just lunged at her."

"She doesn't seem too bothered by it, though."

As people were chiming in, we watched Jack walk over to Star. He stood for a moment before pinning his ears and snaking his head towards her. Star stepped back from the fence, shook, and moved along the fence line, still facing out and away from the group, but she was now directly in front of the round pen and no longer in a corner.

"I think he's trying to get her to go to work." (laughter)

"Maybe he's asking her to join in."

"He's getting after her about something, for sure."

I turned to the group and asked whether this resonated with them. They fell quiet, and an uncomfortable silence descended. I looked at Mike and Katie. They were both looking at the ground. Tiffany, the chief financial officer, finally spoke. "I think we can all resonate a little with this," she began hesitantly. "I know it's hard sometimes when we're doing our thing, and we think we're doing a good job, to have someone come and bark at us for more." A few people nodded. "That took courage to say. Thank you, Tiffany. I see some of you nodding in agreement" I responded. A few more people started to chime in.

> "It can be a little disheartening sometimes when the goal posts keep shifting."
> "I feel like I can never do enough."
> "It would be good to be able to celebrate our achievements before moving on to the next thing."
> "I think our staff feel that pressure from us, too, and it's hard to keep asking things of them without a break, too"
> "I feel like we're constantly chasing and never get ahead enough to take a pause."

As people began to voice their frustrations, the horses went their separate ways in the arena, and one by one rolled in the sand. They stood, shook themselves down, and made their way towards the round pen. They now stood together, close enough to touch muzzles, facing the round pen. Internally, I was doing a little celebratory dance and sending gratitude to the horses, thinking that they had just given a perfect demonstration of how taking a pause, and attending to their own needs, allowed them to come back together as a team with more purpose and cohesion. Bracketing my own response, I asked the group what they noticed about the horses, and what meaning they made of it.

> "I think they just worked out their differences."
> "Star's finally doing what she's being told."
> "I think Jack's got them both in line now."

Ugh. So my interpretation didn't fit theirs, and I knew I needed to let that go. I was aware that we had already taken longer than anticipated for the herd observation. I could feel some restlessness from the group in being confined in the round pen and knew I needed to make a decision about how to move things along. Aha! There's the link. That's how I can join the dots. "What's everyone experiencing right now being in this round pen?" I asked.

> "I feel like Star. I'm being corralled—literally."
> "I feel quite restless."
> "We don't have much choice right now."

The discussion started to flow, and the team began to explore the realities of being in a fast-moving industry, and how Mike felt he had to keep on top of everyone. We explored what it would be like to have more freedom in the moment, and what dangers there would be in reality with the horses if we let everyone out of the round pen. I realized that I needed to let go of our original activity that we had planned. Steering them towards that would reinforce their sense of being corralled. I wanted the group to experience something that required strategic thinking in preparation for their strategy meeting over lunch.

I told them, "I hear clearly that some of you are feeling restless and corralled. I also hear how you want to make sure that we get out of this round pen safely. I want that, too. So your task now is to figure out a strategy where you can stay safe and have everyone leave the round pen in some way to meet and greet the horses.

The group huddled together in the round pen, focused and determined. The horses continued standing together but took a few steps closer to them. The discussion continued as the group considered different ways that they might send only a few of them outside at a time to spread the risk of being outside with the horses.

When asked what difference haltering the horses would make, they recognized that although it would be safer, they would be imposing something on the horses in order to feel better themselves. They also acknowledged that while it would restrict the horses to some degree, it might be the best option they had. I reiterated the safety tips, and suggested that to keep everyone safe, including the horses, that we have no more than four people per horse at a time. It was up to them how they coordinated who went with which horse at any one time.

Julie, Robin, and I haltered the horses, and led them to separate areas around the arena so that we had enough space if the horses needed to move around a little. The group divided themselves up, and the first three groups ventured out of the round pen. I invited those who were still in the round pen to pay attention to how the horses were responding to the people, and vice versa.

Since Star had seemed less interested in engaging with the group initially, I kept a close eye on how she was responding to people approaching her. She was given plenty of rope to move if she needed. Her head was low, and her ears were relaxed. She turned her head towards people as they reached up to stroke her.

It soon became apparent that in their strategic plan of how to meet and greet the horses, the group had not discussed how long each group would take with each horse. Nor had they discussed whether they would rotate to meet all three horses or just the one horse before going back into the round pen. As some people began to walk back to the round pen, others switched to the next horse, and confusion descended.

While Star seemed to willingly engage when there were only four people around her, as a couple more people joined the group, she took a few steps away. I called a time out and asked the group to step away from Star, while checking in with the larger group and questioning their strategy. Having clarified the timing and how they would rotate around the horses, we continued. Star returned to being relaxed as the groups rotated around to meet her. Jack and Misty were enjoying being scratched and loved on, and showed no signs of being over stimulated. The team had successfully rotated through so that everyone had met all three horses. I congratulated them on completing that challenge and asked how they wanted to celebrate.

After a round of high-fives, we continued the session. We now had half an hour left before we needed to wrap up. Having moved away from our original plan of blindfolds, I contemplated whether we had enough time to complete the final part of the activity and decided that if we modified it a little it might work. I asked the participants to step out of the round pen and line up against the fence line, while staying in the groups of four. With the horses on lead, we were able to navigate the space safely.

Checking in with the group, they all expressed delight at meeting the horses up close, and a few of them commented that they wanted more time. I asked if anyone felt drawn to any horse in particular.

> "I liked Jack. He lets you know exactly where he likes being scratched."

"I liked Star. She's sweet and quite introverted. I can relate to that."
"I liked Misty. She's a big girl and just seems super sturdy and reliable."

I asked for six volunteers so that each horse had two people who had picked them as their favorite to work with. I divided the rest of the participants into three groups and explained that they would act as their team's cheer squad. After a quick safety recap and instructions on how to hold the lead rope, I asked the volunteers to position themselves at either end of a line of cones. With horses in place with their new leaders, I gave them the task of weaving through the cones, transitioning their horse to their partner, who would lead them back through the cones to the start. Julie, Robin, and I would take one team each and look out for safety and horse welfare signals during the activity.

The teams got going, and as they practiced weaving through the cones, their cheer squads got louder. Star stopped in her tracks and refused to continue. The participant leading her, Amanda, became flustered. I asked for a time out and asked the group what they thought was happening.

"She's feeling lazy."
"Jack's not making her work, so she's taking advantage."
"She doesn't like being told what to do."

A participant from China, who had not spoken up until this point, covered his ears and said very quietly, "Maybe too loud."
I asked the group if there was anything we could do to support Star. The participants threw out some suggestions: have someone else lead her, pull harder to make it clearer what is expected, let her take a break. They decided that swapping the leader would be the best solution. Amanda handed the lead rope to me and joined the rest of the group as another participant, Joe, stepped forward to take the lead.

Star lifted her head as Joe walked towards us and took a step back. She licked and chewed and shook her head. As he reached us, she turned her head and pinned her ears at him. She was done. I asked Joe to pause and indicated to Julie and Robin that Star needed a break. Taking Star out of the arena, I let her loose in the adjacent paddock and returned to the group.

We reconfigured the activity so that the two who would've been leading Star joined the other two teams. Jack and Misty would now weave the cones three times each, which they did willingly. The next part of the challenge was to see if they could lead the horse through the cones in sync with each other, so that they finished at the same time. I asked the participants who were not leading the horses how they might help the leaders stay connected with each other, and they decided that clapping would keep them in time. The leaders recognized that they also needed to keep an eye out and watch each other as they proceeded through the cones, so that they could match each other's pace.

Off they went! Jack and Misty followed along willingly. Misty's team realized that they had to walk much slower than Jack's team since Misty's stride was so much longer. With a little adjustment along the way, the teams were able to synchronize their steps to complete the task at the same time.

The group immediately asked if more of them could have a turn at leading. Meanwhile, once she had been set loose in the paddock, Star had trotted to the far side, rolled, shook herself off, rolled again, and blew out several times. She was now standing at the arena gate, pawing at the ground. I knew that we were running out of time, and I wanted to give space for the participants to debrief their experience and thank the horses for working with us. I drew the group's attention to Star.

> "Aw, she's feeling left out."
> "She wants to come back to work!"
> "She's had a rest, and she's good to go again."

I walked over to the gate and haltered Star to bring her back into the arena and invited the participants to say their farewells to the horses. I asked them to be mindful of not crowding Star as they said their goodbyes. I directed the participants back to the classroom for our debrief, and thanked Julie, Robin, and the horses before I headed back to meet them.

The Debrief
With such a large group, I had chosen to wrap up the session outside of the arena. I didn't want the horses to be standing around unnecessarily, and I wanted the participants to be able to begin their

transition back into a business environment in readiness for their strategy meeting.

In the debriefing session, I asked the participants the following questions:

1. What did they learn about themselves in that experience?
2. What did they learn about the team?
3. What can they change about how they operate as an organization/team as a result of the experience?

The themes that participants highlighted included:

- How micromanaging can get work done but may not result in a healthy environment: Watching Jack interacting with Star, Mike (CEO) acknowledged that he needed to trust the team more and hover over them less as the lack of freedom means less creativity/productivity.
- How difficult it is to focus on the task at hand when feeling constrained: The participants recognized that feeling corralled by the round pen meant that they rushed through their strategic plan of how to meet and greet the horses, which led to confusion and a feeling of being overwhelmed for both horses and humans. This also linked to how important it is to pause and ask for clarification when dealing with a change of direction.
- How paying attention to signs of burnout before it gets too much can increase productivity: Witnessing how we attended to the horses' welfare, especially with Star, helped to model for the participants a way of giving space to circle back. Seeing how she wanted to re-enter the group after a rest to regroup was a powerful reminder that we can't simply keep going no matter what.
- Slowing down to speed up: By taking the time to attend to potential burnout and feeling overwhelmed, productivity can be increased. Rather than having to overload staff to pick up the slack, going at a pace that prevents burnout would be in everyone's interest. Star being taken out of the arena meant that Jack and Misty had to work extra hard, taking on more people and weaving an extra line of cones.
- Taking time to notice the small achievements and celebrating goals along the way is crucial to continued

engagement. Jack and Misty's willingness to engage was matched by the love and attention they received. The participants appreciated how once the task was completed, and they asked for more from the horses, it was a reflection of the organizational culture of not pausing to celebrate an achievement. By not succumbing to the request, we emphasized taking care of the staff (in this case the horses) versus pushing for increased productivity.

- Need to adapt the way they communicated depending on who they were dealing with: Witnessing how the horses reacted to what was being asked of them highlighted the need for them, as leaders within the organization, to be more cognizant of issues of diversity. With such an international team, the organization needed to be more attuned to cultural differences that arise.

This case study demonstrates the fine line we tread as practitioners of taking care of the needs of the horses and providing clients with the experiential learning that they are seeking. For me, it's important that I advocate for the horses every time. Handling any disappointment or change of direction with the participants can often be part of the learning. Modeling a compassionate and relational approach for all involved often brings about deeper reflection from participants. This session lasted two hours with the horses, and so much happened within it that even in re-telling the events, there is so much detail that is missed.

Existential themes of isolation and freedom were evident throughout this session. Working phenomenologically while paying attention to the relational shifts between participants and horses is much more difficult with a large group. The temptation to interpret how the horses are showing up is stronger, and bracketing our own opinions becomes harder. There were moments during this session where I felt frustrated with the CEO, and moments where I really wanted to share my interpretation of what the horses were doing. If I had not bracketed both of those, the participants would not have experienced the aha moments for themselves. I would simply have been telling them my opinions, and that's not what they were there to learn.

There were multiple choice points throughout the session. When one participant commented on the round pen being like a UFC boxing octagon, I wondered how that linked to his experience of being part of the team. My sense was that there were many unresolved conflicts in the team that may have come to the surface if I had gone down that path. Jack's behavior towards Star could have highlighted conflicts that may have needed moments of pause to resolve, which would have circled us back to the session objectives. When Misty kicked the cones away in the arena, I was curious about what it meant to see her making space for herself. When a participant noticed Jack had taken his time before engaging, I wondered how that connected to what they needed to learn in the session.

In the moments following Tiffany's courageous comments, I could have asked what it was like to have a frank discussion in the moment. This may have prompted them to notice how much they all had in common. The reality is that we never know what meaning participants will make, and what connections they might draw from the experience. My belief is that all roads lead to Rome, and by staying present to what is unfolding, something would have come from any of those choices that would have led us back to our session objectives.

While we had an activity planned out, we adapted to the situation in each moment, and adjusted the plan as the session unfolded. I felt confident that the themes that were emerging would result in the participants meeting the session objectives that we had set. This was confirmed in the debriefing session and became a focus for their strategy meeting.

In sessions like these, I often have the feeling of walking a tightrope while spinning and balancing a dozen plates. Keeping track of what participants say while noticing the more subtle non-verbal cues, keeping track of horse welfare and safety, following the themes that emerge and tying them into the session objectives is a lot to hold. I believe that holding that space is only possible because of the incredible partners I work with, horses and human. At the end of an event like this, I always feel so much gratitude for the team around me. It's why I make sure that participants offer thanks to everyone involved on their way out of the arena, because it's only possible to run a team-building event when we can model teamwork ourselves.

Case Study 4: Where's Your Hula-Hoop?

Several years ago, I was asked to run a one-time event for a group of teenage girls. I knew one of the girl's parents, and during a night out, they had mentioned that their daughter and her friends had been discussing how difficult it was to fend off unwanted sexual attention. They were worried that the girls didn't know how to say no to sexual advances and wanted to provide them with some skills and confidence to stand their ground. This particular group of young women were all between 16 and 19 years old and part of an anxiety support group. They had been attending the group for some time and had started to meet socially. They were all navigating the teenage angst of potential romantic relationships. My friends had spoken to the other parents, and they were keen to set up an EFL session for the girls to explore this topic.

The group of five young women arrived at the barn excited to spend time with the horses. Two of them had some previous horseback riding experience, but the others had never been around horses before. So I started with a safety briefing and the HERD safety agreement before leading them through a grounding exercise.

We began by gathering outside the paddock where the horses were grazing, and I invited them to pay attention to their surroundings. I asked them to name five things that they could see, four things they could touch, three things they could hear, two things they could smell, and one thing they could taste. We focused on taking in a few deep breaths, planting our feet hip-distance apart, and exhaling fully.

Beginning with some herd observation, I asked the girls to pay attention to what they noticed about the horses. The horses were grazing in the paddock, standing closely together. As we watched them, Arrow walked over to where Cheyenne was grazing and sniffed her back end. The girls giggled. Cheyenne turned and looked at Arrow before walking away. Arrow then walked towards Reba with his neck outstretched. Before he could get close enough to sniff or touch her, Reba walked away. Arrow turned and faced Cheyenne and approached her from behind once more. Again, he sniffed her back end, and again, she walked away. The horses repeated this dance another couple of times before Arrow stopped, shook his body, and dropped his head back down to graze. He was now standing farther away from the other two horses than before. After a couple of minutes, Cheyenne walked over to Arrow and stood next to him. He turned and sniffed her, and she walked away. I asked the participants what they were aware of.

> "Arrow keeps annoying the girls."
> "He's pushing them around."
> "He's such a boy!"
> "Cheyenne's teasing him."
> "Arrow's flirting with them."

I was curious that they hadn't mentioned him stopping to graze before Cheyenne approached him, but I let that go and followed their figure of interest. I asked them what the difference was for them between flirting and teasing. Melanie, the oldest in the group, said that flirting was playful but teasing was mean. The others nodded in agreement. "I mean, like, teasing is when you don't really wanna talk with someone but you want the attention, or you're bored so you'll put something out there to see what reaction you'll get," said Penny. "But you're only interested until something better comes along. People do that all the time. It's so annoying."

I said that it sounded like they had all experienced something similar and didn't like being teased that way. "How do you know if someone is teasing rather than flirting?" I asked.

"Well, if they're teasing you, sometimes they'll just ghost you in the middle of a conversation. Like, they'll just stop texting all of a sudden," said Emily.

"What about when they're flirting? What's the difference then?" I asked.

The girls grew quiet and pondered for a moment. Meanwhile, Arrow had made his way over to the fence. He stretched his neck over and nudged Melanie. She stepped towards him and scratched his neck. "Oh, you're such a handsome boy!" she exclaimed. "You like this spot, don't you?" she said, as she scratched him under his chin. Arrow lifted his head up and stretched. Melanie, pausing to consider the question I'd just asked about flirting, momentarily stopped scratching him. Arrow dropped his head and nudged Melanie on her shoulder, pushing her off balance, and she stumbled to the side. I watched as she gathered herself up and returned to scratching Arrow. Instead of continuing to scratch under his chin as before, Melanie reached up to his neck. Arrow turned and nudged her, once again sending her off balance.

Me: What's happening for you right now, Melanie?

Melanie (laughing): He keeps pushing me. Does he not want me to scratch him? I thought he was enjoying that.

Me: What might that mean for you if he did or didn't like it?

Melanie: Well, if he doesn't like it. I'll stop.

Me: I notice that you're still standing next to him, and he's turned and nudged you on your shoulders a couple more times while we've been talking. What's that like for you?

Melanie: Well, I didn't know if he wanted me to leave him alone or keep scratching, so I stayed.

Me: What's it like for the rest of you to watch what's happening between Melanie and Arrow?

Penny: I think he's just being a boy. I don't think he knows what he wants.

Emily: He looked like he was enjoying it. Maybe he's trying to tell you where he wants to be scratched?

In this moment, I was aware that I had a number of options. T the figures that were emerging were a) how to navigate a relationship when you wanted something from another; b) how to navigate a relationship when the other is being unclear, or c) how to distinguish between what you want and what someone else is expecting. These were all ripe areas for discussion and tied in with the purpose of the session. I trusted that whichever direction I followed, it would lead to something meaningful for the group.

> **Me:** So I hear there are a few things that might be going on here. I'm curious about what you want between you and Arrow right now, Melanie?
>
> **Melanie:** I want to keep petting him if he wants me to.

Ugh. How hard it is to be a teenage girl! In that split second, I wanted to take Melanie by her shoulders and look her in the eyes to let her know that her wishes are just as important as anyone else's, and that she would learn in time that her voice matters. The existential angst of needing to belong, loved, and validated for who they are was so present in each of these young women. The yearning to be seen, combined with the fear of isolation, is an existential journey that we all experience. At 19, it often feels like the choice between life or death. I resonated deeply with this young woman, but I also knew that I needed to bracket all of that pain and angst that I recognized. And while I knew that at 19 I had struggled with the same dilemmas these girls were experiencing, this was their own journey. So instead, I reiterated my question about what it was like for the rest of the group to see what was happening between Melanie and Arrow.

> **Penny:** You should move to see if he'll follow you. Then you'll know what he wants.
> **Emily:** Yeah, but only if you want him to follow you.
> **Me:** That's a good point, Emily. How do we let others know if we want to be followed, or not?

Melanie stood still, looking down at the ground. I got the feeling that the attention was getting to be too much for her and didn't want to push her beyond her window of tolerance. If this was an EFP session, I could have taken this line of inquiry deeper, but this was an EFL session, and I needed to stay within my scope of practice. So I switched gears, focused on the rest of the group, and offered them the opportunity to go into the paddock with the horses.

The activity I had planned for the session was a simple experiential exercise using hula-hoops. I gave each participant a hula-hoop before going into the paddock. I encouraged each of them to hold it however they wanted and told them as long as they didn't throw it around the paddock, they could do what they wanted with them. I invited the girls to go and meet the horses with their hula-hoops, paying attention to the safety elements that we had discussed at the beginning.

Three of the participants immediately put the hula-hoops over their heads and held them around their waists. I noticed that Penny was standing in the center of the hoop, with her hands stretched out on either side as she held it in place. Emily had placed the hoop against her back, positioning her hands slightly behind her hips to hold it. Simone held her hoop with her left hand on her hip, so that the hoop was sticking out to the side and slightly slanted towards the ground. Melanie and Chantelle had decided not to stand inside their hoops and were holding them flat against their sides.

Arrow looked up as the group approached the herd and immediately began to walk over to Emily. With her hoop stuck out in front of her, Emily stood still as Arrow approached. He stretched his neck towards her, sniffed the hoop, grabbed it with his lips and nodded his head. Emily laughed. "Let go of my hula-hoop," she said, as she gripped the hoop tighter and pulled it away from him while taking a step back. Arrow turned away and walked over to Penny. His chest bumped against the edge of her hoop as he reached across to the middle where she stood and sniffed her shoulder, making her giggle. "Hey, that tickles!" she said and took a step away.

Meanwhile, Cheyenne had walked over to Simone, who had turned to face her so that her hula-hoop was now stretching out behind her as she held it with one hand while gently stroking Cheyenne with her free hand. Reba had made her way across the paddock to Melanie and Chantelle, who had been standing close to each other holding their hula-hoops flat against their sides. Reba walked straight between them, causing them to step away from each other to make space for her. I watched as Chantelle walked around Reba in order to stand next to Melanie again. Reba turned and walked between them again. Once more, Chantelle walked around Reba to re-establish her position next to Melanie. Again, Reba turned and walked between them.

There was so much going on! I now had multiple interactions between the horses and participants that were capturing my attention. Should I follow my curiosity about the positioning of the hula-hoops? Should I explore the way that, with the exception of Simone, they had all stepped away from the horses? Should I focus on what it was like to have attention from the horses? And, what kind of attention? Is it something they were enjoying or not? If not, how were they communicating that? I was also keeping an eye on issues of safety, and wondered how that might also relate to the challenges these young women might be experiencing out in the wider world.

The goal of the session was to help the participants gain clarity about boundaries and, by doing so, increase their confidence to reject unwanted advances. The horses were all doing an incredible job of highlighting how the participants naturally responded to being approached. I was interested in how they were experiencing this process with the horses. "I notice that you're all holding your hula-hoops in different ways. How has that impacted how you are interacting with the horses?" I asked.

Chantelle didn't think that the hula-hoop made much difference as she was only holding hers and not standing inside it. Melanie agreed. Emily liked the feeling of being inside the hoop as it acted as a barrier when Arrow got too close. Penny had fun playing with Arrow when he reached inside the hoop towards her but liked that he didn't get too close. Simone was resting her head on Cheyenne's shoulder when she responded, "I moved my hoop around so that I could get closer to her," she said with a smile.

> **Me:** What was it like for you to move your hoop?
> **Simone:** It was fine. I chose to because I wanted to get closer to her.
> **Me:** What do the rest of you notice about the difference between Simone and Cheyenne's interaction compared to what you experienced?
> **Penny:** I was waiting for Arrow to decide how he wanted to greet me.
> **Emily:** I think I did that too. I told him what I didn't like, though, when he grabbed my hula-hoop!
> **Melanie:** Well, me and Chantelle didn't even have a barrier up at all, so Reba just walked all over us.
> **Chantelle:** No, but I did try to tell her I didn't want her to stand between us. I kept trying to stand next to you again— also because I thought you were a bit scared of her.
> **Melanie:** Thanks. I am a bit.

I asked the group when they were feeling scared or uncertain of how to handle being approached by others, what they could do. The conversation flowed into how they could pay more attention to what they wanted, stand their ground and say no, and/or ask for support. As we processed what had emerged, we had all gravitated towards Simone and Cheyenne, who were still standing together, so that we were including them in the circle we had created. Arrow and Reba were standing behind Penny, just beyond the circle.

> **Me:** I notice that while we've been talking, Arrow and Reba have been standing outside our circle. What do you make of that?
> **Emily:** I think they know we were talking about them intruding on us earlier, and now they're respecting our space.
> **Chantelle:** I think so too. Reba looks sad.
> **Simone:** Even if she's sad because you said no, it doesn't mean you have to give in, right?
> **Me:** Absolutely. You have the right to choose how you interact.

Penny: But what if we want to interact, just not the way they want to?

Simone: Then you show them. I'm snuggling with Cheyenne because we both want to. But if she's rude, then I'd let her know. Not that she'd be rude, of course, because she's lovely.

Me: So how might we let Arrow and Reba know how we want to interact with them in a way that's okay for all of us?

Emily: We could see if they want to join our circle?

The group agreed to create space for the horses to join us and stepped back. After a few moments, Reba stepped up into the gap next to Penny. Arrow walked up, paused at the edge of the circle, and promptly walked forward and positioned himself in the center of the group. The participants laughed and joked that it was typical for a boy to push his way through.

Me: So what choices do we have right now?

Simone: We could ask him to back up to where we want him.

Emily: That's a good idea. How do we do that?

Penny, one of the participants with previous horse experience, volunteered to show the others how to ask a horse to back up. She stepped forward and positioned herself in front of Arrow, moved into his space and tapped him on his chest while asking him to back up. Arrow stood his ground. Penny tried again to no avail. "I guess I'm going to have to really mean it," she said, "Arrow, I want you to back up." This time, as she pushed on his chest, she stepped forward into his space, and he took a few steps backwards to the edge of the circle. "Thank you" said Penny, as she reclaimed her space in the group.

In wrapping up the session, the participants were able to articulate the importance of being clear in their communicating when they don't want to engage if another approaches, and that they have the right to choose how they want to engage. They became more aware of how their fear of upsetting the other meant that they ended up tolerating advances that they were uncomfortable with and/or resulting in unsafe situations. Witnessing Simone's connection with Cheyenne helped them to understand that the type of relationships they want need to be a mutual engagement of respectful boundaries and consideration.

This session demonstrates the importance of staying in the present moment while zooming in and zooming out in order to track the interactions between horses and participants. By working phenomenologically to bracket my own feelings in order not to impose my own agenda on the participants' experience, I allowed the young women to draw meaning for themselves from their interactions with the horses. Being mindful of scope of practice in moments when participants are on the edge of their window of tolerance allows us to draw attention away from them and redirect the group, while holding space for the participant to self-regulate. Holding an awareness of the existential themes of freedom and isolation that emerged gave depth to the experience.

For me, this session will always be close to my heart as I have been privileged to witness the lasting impact of this experience for my friends' daughter. A few years after the event, I saw the young woman, who was in her early 20s by then. After regaling me with her stories from college, she turned to me solemnly and said, "Miss Veronica, do you remember that time you had me and my friends come over to your barn, and we did that thing with the horses and hula-hoops? I think about that every time I meet a new guy I like. I ask myself how I'm holding my hula-hoop with him in a way that I want and can get respect from him. I've told so many of my friends at college about that that they now ask me where's my hula-hoop all the time!"

Case Study 5: I'll Be There for You

Carol had heard about me from a friend who had attended a women's retreat that I had offered a few months previously. Her daughter, Laura, had been diagnosed with diabetes when she was eight years old. Laura was now in her senior year in high school and was preparing to leave for college. She was a straight-A student, had been accepted into her first-choice college as a pre-vet student, and was excited about her future. Carol, on the other hand, was worried that Laura was not ready for the responsibility of living on her own, particularly with regard to monitoring her blood-sugar levels and diabetes management. Carol wanted Laura to attend a college closer to home so that she could be there in case of emergencies. Laura was adamant that she would be fine, believing that she would be able to manage herself. She was angry that her mother couldn't trust her.

Laura had been riding horses since she was eleven years old, so Carol thought that a series of EFL sessions might help Laura identify the areas where she would be willing to allow Carol to help her without limiting her sense of freedom. During our phone conversation, Carol had initially suggested that Laura attend a series of individual sessions with me. After listening to her case, I realized that it might be more helpful for them to come together.

In this case, I was very aware of the fine line between EFL and EFP. Given the challenges that mother and daughter were both facing, I knew that I would need to attend to my scope of practice very carefully. Carol was a licensed professional counselor and knew that Laura would balk at the idea that her mom was "dragging her to therapy" and was very clear that she had positioned these sessions as "life skills sessions" so Laura could focus on learning how to transition into adult living and she could learn to let go. While Laura was not entirely enthusiastic about the idea, it was the latter objective that had persuaded her to attend.

We had agreed on a series of eight sessions. At the start, Laura had been resistant to the idea that she was not responsible enough to manage her health. Carol had spent a lot of time attempting to provide evidence of the nuanced symptoms that she was constantly on alert for in her daughter that she did not think Laura was aware of. Laura had challenged her with counterarguments around how she was perfectly capable of taking care of herself during the school day without her mother's help. They had gone back and forth, and the sessions had been full of tension.

In the first few sessions, my horses barely paid any attention to them. When we entered the pasture, they would walk away from us, often standing facing the opposite direction. Carol and Laura interpreted these moments in different ways. Carol thought it meant that it reflected how Laura was reacting to her—not listening and ignoring her advice. Laura had found meaning in seeing the horses taking care of themselves.

In our third session, Reba, my chestnut mare, decided to stay closer to us after the other two horses had walked away. Reba approached Laura and was sniffing her neck. Laura responded by giggling and reciprocating the affection with scratching Reba on her chest. I watched as Reba continued to sniff Laura, down her neck and shoulders and all the way down her arm. She dipped her head lower and sniffed down Laura's leg and stopped mid-thigh and nudged her with her nose. Laura giggled, shifted her weight, and continued to scratch Reba on her chest. Reba nudged her again on her thigh.

I asked Laura what was happening. She shrugged her shoulders and looked down at Reba, who had now shifted her focus to sniffing Laura's belly. "I don't know," said Laura, "but she seems to be sniffing me where I inject myself." Suddenly, she looked at her watch and quickly looked at Carol, eyes wide. Without a word, Carol walked briskly out of the pasture towards their car. Laura turned and followed, calling over her shoulder at me, "We'll be right back."

Confused, I watched as Carol handed Laura a black pouch as she slid into the passenger seat. A moment later, Laura re-emerged, handed the pouch back to Carol, and they walked back into the paddock. Reba had walked over to the gate, watching them the whole time. "Your horse is a genius" said Carol, "I deliberately stopped myself from reminding Laura this morning to check her blood sugar levels. I've been trying to back off like we'd agreed."

Apparently, Reba's sniffing had prompted Laura that she had yet to check her blood sugar. As it turned out, her blood levels were within range and all was well. As we continued the session, Reba stayed close by. Laura was able to feel Reba as a source of support rather than interference, unlike her mother. Carol was able to see that perhaps others might be able to step in to help. This was a turning point for them, and we began to focus on what steps they both needed to take in order for both of them to feel supported.

Over the next couple of sessions, the other two horses began to interact more, but Reba was always close by. We had focused on the idea of mutual partnership rather than control, experimenting with walking with Reba off lead. We played with the idea of assimilating novel experiences through introducing the giant soccer ball to Reba, and we had spent time simply sharing space with the horses in the pasture without expectations. This last experience was impactful for both mother and daughter as it reinforced the idea that it was possible to be connected through being with each other rather than Laura feeling that she had to meet expectations or Carol feeling that she had to actively monitor Laura. Through these experiences, they had both deepened their relationship with Reba.

In their final session, I introduced the idea of a mounted experience. Knowing that Laura was a skilled rider, I had imagined that she could get on Reba and go for a walk around the arena while Carol watched. I had in my mind that this might be symbolic of Laura leaving home for college and thought it might be a good way to end our time together. I had imagined that this would be an affirmative celebration of Laura's independence and Carol's acceptance of her ability to take responsibility for herself. That was my plan.

We began the session by reviewing what they had learned from their time with the horses. Laura was pleased that Carol had begun to trust her more and was feeling confident about her ability to take care of herself away from home. Carol admitted that while she had seen improvements and a high degree of effort from Laura, as her mother it would be impossible not to worry.

As we talked, Reba walked over to us and stood between mother and daughter. I introduced my idea of a mounted experience, which was met with enthusiasm, and suggested that we lead Reba into the barn to get her ready. As with most mounted experiences I offer, I had planned on using a bareback pad on Reba. I knew that Laura had ridden bareback before, so I wasn't concerned about her.

Carol and Laura groomed Reba together, chatting about how excited they felt about the activity. They worked well together, handing each other grooming tools, stepping away to give space to each other, and were at ease in each other's company. Reba was relaxed and responsive to the attention she was receiving. I stepped in to put the bareback pad on Reba, explaining as I went that I wanted to Laura to feel more movement under her.

> **Carol:** So, you're not going to be putting an actual saddle on her? Is that safe?
> **Laura:** Mom, it'll be fine! I know how to ride, and you know I've ridden bareback before.
> **Carol:** But that just seems so...exposing.
> **Laura** (laughing): Mom, it's called freedom! I think you should get on instead of me so you can let go a bit more.

Carol's eyes widened. Laura and I looked at each other and smiled. I told them that this could be an option if that's what they wanted to do and assured Carol that we would be there to support her every step of the way. Laura seemed particularly excited about the idea of her mom getting on instead of her. "We don't even need to walk anywhere, you could just get on," she said. Carol looked at me warily and asked me what I thought.

> **Me:** Laura's right. We could just explore you getting on and standing still and see how that feels. If you feel comfortable

with that, we could go on a little walk. I can walk alongside you while Laura leads Reba. You'll be on the lead rope the whole time, whatever we do. And, you don't have to do it at all if you don't want to.

Laura: It's not like you've not ridden before, Mom. I think you'll like it. I'll be here the whole time.

Carol (smiling at Laura): You know what, kiddo? I'll do it. I trust you.

Laura led Reba to the mounting block and waited. I encouraged Carol to take her time and take a few deep breaths before stepping up to the block. As she stepped up onto the block, Reba turned towards her. Quietly, Carol asked Reba if it was okay to get on. She stroked her on her withers and slowly swung her leg over and gently sat down. Grinning at Laura, Carol asked her to take a few steps forward.

The theme throughout the sessions with Carol and Laura was one of trust. In debriefing the mounted experience, Carol acknowledged that it took a leap of faith for her to get on Reba, and that it was only possible because of the relationship that they had built with her in previous sessions. Carol was also surprised in the moment that she genuinely felt that she could trust Laura to lead Reba, drawing a parallel in how this meant that she could trust her to lead her own life. Laura was ecstatic that her mom had trusted her as she felt confident that she was able to take the responsibility of leading Reba. This translated into her sense of confidence in herself moving forward, while knowing that her mom would always be available for support.

This case study demonstrates how to introduce a mounted experience into an EFL session. The act of building a relationship between the participants and the horses is critical to the process. It is important to be clear about the purpose of mounted work. In this scenario, while I had a different idea in mind, I was able to hold the framework of how the mounted experience would impact on the relationship, and flow with what the participants needed in the moment to adapt the session. What transpired was clearly more profound and impactful than what I had in mind, once again, reinforcing the importance of letting go of a set agenda.

It's not about the activity. It's all about relationships!

EFL Case Studies: Conclusion

These case studies exemplify the HERD EFL Model through the continuous attention to the moment-by-moment unfolding of the relational dynamics between horses and participants. In recounting each case study, there are many more details that have fallen into the background so that the figure of phenomenological inquiry and attention to the I–Thou moments of the session could be highlighted. Each case study demonstrates the three stages of the HERD EFL Model through meeting (clients, participants, and horses), relating (here and now, what and how, I–Thou), and integrating (learning gained).

By keeping within our scope of practice and attending to the participants' experiences, we can provide long-lasting, impactful, and transformative learning. By partnering with our horses in a way that allows them the freedom to engage on their own terms, without jeopardizing standards of safety, we can rest assured that the connections participants make with the horses are authentic. The beauty of stepping into sessions with a flexible session plan means that we can meet our participants where they are rather than presume to know what they need. The experience of authentic connection in each moment is where learning takes place.

It's not about the activity. It's all about relationships!

Chapter 13

Equine-Facilitated Psychotherapy Case Studies

This chapter aims to immerse you in the lives of a diverse range of clients I have worked with over the years. Their personal details have been altered to preserve their anonymity and confidentiality, but the essence of their journeys remains intact. Some of the names of the horses have changed; others appear as themselves. The case studies are discussed in terms of the HERD EFP Model to clearly illustrate the philosophical and theoretical foundations and demonstrate the wide-ranging clinical applications of this approach. These cases also offer readers insight into the organic nature of how a session unfolds; they are narrated in a way that allows for flow of reading the story while also providing notes for a "behind the scenes" glimpse at the thought process behind each choice point. Readers are encouraged to think outside the box for alternative ways to respond in each situation to enhance their own learning.

Case Study 1: Bow and Arrow

Virginia was referred to me for EFP through an outpatient eating disorders clinic by her individual therapist. She had been in and out of residential treatment programs over the last 10 years. At 32 years old, she was now in a committed relationship and was hoping to get married. Virginia wanted to have children but was aware that she needed to break out of her destructive cycle of bulimia nervosa in order to have a healthy pregnancy. This provided her with a powerful motivation to change her behaviors, but she was still struggling to implement the changes she needed to make. Her bingeing/purging cycle consisted of secret binges in the middle of the night, mostly on weekends, followed by excessive exercise and laxatives. While her weight had not fluctuated too much, and she was within normal weight ranges, her blood work showed high cholesterol and high-risk markers for Type II diabetes. Virginia felt ashamed of her secret binges and reported bouts of depression following her more extreme binge/purge cycles.

Bulimia nervosa is one of the most common types of eating disorders and is an increasing concern within the mental health field. With an estimated prevalence of 1% to 2% in women and 0.5% in men, it is also often underreported and misdiagnosed. Characterized by consuming large quantities of food, followed by compensating for this by the bingeing, many sufferers are undiagnosed due to being within normal body weight. Symptoms include excessive eating (often in secret), obsession with body weight, feelings of shame around food, self-induced vomiting and/or starvation, excessive exercise, and abuse of laxatives, diuretics, or diet pills.

Virginia had been experiencing this cycle of shame since her teenage years. As a member of the cheer squads through high school and college, she had been surrounded by others who had normalized these behaviors. The competitive environment and mutual scrutiny embedded within the cheerleading culture had kept Virginia feeling isolated while also providing a sense of belonging. This existential dilemma of feeling alone in the world while seemingly connected was a theme that recurred throughout our time together.

Sharing Space
In her first session with the horses, Virginia arrived after a particularly challenging day at work. I watched as she got out of her car and hurried over to the gate where I was waiting. I invited her into the barn to complete the required paperwork before heading out to the horses. Looking at Virginia, I noticed that I was holding my breath, so intentionally took a couple of deep, audible breaths to center myself. I asked her to pay attention to her own breathing and invited her to join me in taking some deep breaths together before heading into the pasture to meet the horses. Virginia responded by taking a small, staccato, breath, which she then held for a couple of beats before exhaling. I continued to take big, deep breaths, and noticed that Virginia's breathing deepened slightly as she watched me breathe. Gradually, she dropped her shoulders and took one big breath and exhaled.

After going through our safety protocol, I gave Virginia some time to observe the herd grazing in the pasture. It was a glorious sun-drenched evening with a cool breeze, and the horses had just been turned out for the night. My two mares were standing close together, eating peacefully, while my gelding was by himself in the far corner of the field, dozing in the sunshine.

> **Me:** What's happening for you right now?
> **Virginia:** I feel sad. I'm looking at that horse over there all by himself. It reminds me of how I am when I'm watching other people eat.
> **Me:** Where do you feel that sadness in your body?
> **Virginia:** It's like a numbness in my core.
> **Me:** What happens if we focus on that a little?
> **Virginia:** It gets heavier. Usually when I feel like this, I start thinking about bingeing.
> **Me:** I notice you're still looking at Arrow over there.
> **Virginia:** Yes, I don't want him to be on his own.
> **Me:** How would you like to be with him?
> **Virginia:** I'd like to go and stand next to him, so he knows he's not alone.

Virginia's process of sharing space with the herd had emerged. In feeling her embodied experience of being with others while feeling isolated, I was curious to know what she desired. Virginia walked over to Arrow. Stopping about ten feet away from him, she looked down at her feet and began to cry. I was aware that her primary therapist had told me that Virginia struggled with allowing herself to cry and/or show any signs of vulnerability around others. I wanted to give her time to feel her tears, particularly as she had mentioned a feeling of numbness moments before. This moved us into the second stage of the HERD EFP Model of release and expand.

Release and Expand

Working from a phenomenological approach may invoke the actuality of experiences for clients who have become numb to their destructive process. The interactions with the horses may act as metaphors for clients to rest their experiences on and/or translate to experiencing the actual relationship that is emerging. The horse's willingness to engage in relationship often challenges a client's perception of self-worth. Within the process of bulimia, there exists a paradox in the client's own feelings of worthlessness that drives them towards thinness, believing that once thinness is achieved, they would be worthy to live, love, and survive. Yet, it is the client's striving for that same thinness that will potentially cause death.

Many individuals suffering from bulimia nervosa become stuck in this cycle of shame and feelings of unworthiness. Rules and routines are often mixed with impulsive, and sometimes dissociative, binges that reinforce a sense of failure of one's ability to maintain order. Living with bulimia nervosa is a lonely existence. Social engagements, which often involve communal eating, are fraught with anxiety and purposefully avoided. Virginia had become isolated from her peers and family, further confirming her view of herself as unworthy of attention. In the world of social media, this existential isolation is increasingly overcome by seeking out online support groups to find "thinspiration" that results in peer pressure like no other. Virginia's history of being part of a cheer squad had led her to seek out support, but this had resulted in her replicating the unhealthy dynamics of peer pressure and competitiveness of her cheer squad days. This was the lifespace that contextualized her way of being in the world.

In my experience, clients with bulimia nervosa often find it easier to numb their bodily sensations than to allow them to surface. Bingeing helps to deflect from the physical sensations that hint at emotion. Acknowledging Virginia's tears, and allowing for her to sink into that experience, supported her ability to release some of her rules about not showing her vulnerability. I wanted to give her space for that release.

After a few moments, I asked Virginia what she was experiencing. She explained that it had seemed so simple to offer the horse some comfort when she thought he was lonely, but she realized that when she felt isolated, she found it hard to reach out for support. She brushed away her tears as she spoke and took a few deep breaths. As she exhaled, Arrow walked over to her and started sniffing her shoulder. She reached out to pet him on his neck. I invited her to spend some time getting to know him and watched as she moved to his side and leaned her head and chest on him. Arrow stood still as they both breathed deeply.

Deepening
This experience of being supported in a more embodied way moved us into the deepening stage of the HERD EFP Model. As Virginia took a step closer to Arrow and put more weight on him, he turned his head towards her and wrapped his neck around her. Virginia

continued to cry. I gave them space to experience the moment between them and watched as she reached her arms around his neck and hugged him tight. After a few moments, Virginia straightened herself up and exhaled deeply. Arrow dropped his head to the ground and began to graze.

Virginia continued to stroke Arrow on the neck as he grazed. After two or three bites, Arrow took a step forward, lifted his head towards Virginia, and then continued to graze. Virginia adjusted herself and followed him. Again, Arrow moved after a few bites, lifted his head towards Virginia, and she followed and continued to pet him. This dance was repeated several more times. I waited and watched. Virginia was immersed in the experience between her and Arrow, and I wanted to give them time to connect. After a few minutes, I noticed that we were now in close proximity to the two mares who had continued to graze peacefully the whole time we were with Arrow. We were now approaching the penultimate stage of coming home to relationships in the HERD EFP Model.

Come Home to Relationships

> **Me:** What are you aware of now?
> **Virginia** (looking up and around her, laughing): I didn't realize we'd traveled so far across the field. I had no idea that we were so close to the other two horses!
> **Me:** What do you make of that?
> **Virginia:** I think he just needed permission to start eating with the others.
> **Me:** How does that resonate with you?
> **Virginia:** I need support to be able to eat without feeling ashamed. I need to reach out for that support somehow. I'd like to be able to get to the point where I can eat with others in public without constantly feeling anxious that I'm being judged. Or judging myself.

As she spoke, the mares began to walk towards us, and Arrow turned to face them. The mares, Reba and Cheyenne, stopped about 50 feet away from us, with their heads low and ears forward. Slowly, they dipped their heads in unison and began to graze in front of us. Arrow stood still while facing them but did not resume his grazing.

Me: What's happening for you now?

Virginia: I'm making up a story in my head about how the mean girls have come over to judge Arrow, and that's why he's not eating.

Me: How would you like to support Arrow?

Virginia: Well, I don't want to lead him away because I don't want him to feel like he has to be on his own to get what he needs. But I also don't want him to feel judged. I don't know!! This is how I feel all the time.

Integration

Virginia's eyes became tearful once more. Reba lifted her head and walked towards her. Arrow stood his ground and stretched his neck out towards Reba and sniffed. I was about to remind Virginia to be mindful of safety and spacing around the horses, when she held out both her hands, one palm facing towards each horse and said, "Okay, that's enough now. Don't get so close". The horses both backed up a step.

Me: How do you feel right now?

Virginia (with her hands still up): I feel good actually. I don't know what prompted me to do that, other than remembering what you'd said about safety earlier. I didn't want them to get too close to me. I didn't think that they would respond to me. But it was instinct on my part, I guess. I mean, I could've walked away, I suppose.

Me: What difference would that make for you?

Virginia: I don't want to walk away anymore. I want to face my fears and live more fully. I want to have a baby, and that means that I have to change. I also know it's freaking me out that being pregnant will change my body and trigger my eating disorder stuff. But I really want to face this head-on and not run away from it.

I shared with Virginia that I was about to remind her of safety when she held up her hands. I wanted to acknowledge that she had stepped in to take care of herself without being prompted. This resonated for her in how she wanted to keep herself safe from being triggered into her eating disorder. How she had interacted with the horses in that moment provided her with a sense of solidity within herself that could support her ability to hold clearer boundaries with her eating habits. As we talked, Virginia walked towards the horses. Approaching each one in turn, she reached up and stroked them on their neck and shoulders. The horses each paused from their grazing and turned towards her before dropping their heads to continue to eat. After greeting each one, she turned to me and said, "They're not the mean girls. I'm the mean girl to myself. I just need to catch myself when I'm beating myself up. Arrow can take care of himself and so can I, but sometimes it's nice to have the support."

This process of integration allowed Virginia to begin her journey towards reaching out for support from her partner when she felt the urge to binge. Instead of isolating herself and numbing her bodily senses to her need for connection and feeding the emptiness within her through bingeing, she slowly began to feel the sensations of fullness both physically and psychologically.

Ultimately, Virginia's story is a classic rendition of the importance of relationships and echoes the existential–humanistic and Gestalt principle that it is the relationship that heals. This case study offers the practitioner a glimpse of the depth of work possible while holding the framework of the HERD EFP Model. It also highlights the power of the phenomenological and the I–Thou approach.

It is imperative for practitioners to understand that the HERD Model is not a linear or static process. Through the lived experiences of our clients, it would be tempting to track the progress of clients based on which stage of the model they are in. In truth, some clients may appear to move through the whole cycle within one session, while others remain in one stage for a number of months or dance between the stages. This does not mean that one is making more progress than the other; instead, we pay attention to the insight gained and the relational shifts that emerge from each stage.

This case study clearly demonstrates the impact of staying with the process rather than introducing a pre-determined activity into the session. By paying attention to what emerged between Virginia and the horses, each new interaction became the figure of the moment and, as such, the "activity" in the process. From Virginia's initial observation of the horses and our intentionally relational act of breathing together, to Virginia walking with Arrow across the field, and her instinctive response when the horses came too close for comfort, we focused on the actual relational shifts and her growing awareness of her way of being in the world. This allowed Virginia to access her own embodied experience and find a clearer sense of how she could integrate these experiences into her everyday life. By staying with a descriptive and phenomenological stance in my observations of her interactions throughout the session, Virginia was able to make meaning of the encounter for herself.

For me, one of the most challenging aspects of being a therapist sometimes is in not knowing how the story plays out for many of my clients. There are some who will forever stand out in my memory, and each time my thoughts land on them, I take a moment to send out my heartfelt gratitude to them along with the continued hope that they have found a way to thrive in the world. Virginia's journey is one that I hold dearly in my heart, as her story captures the essence of my philosophical foundations: that by opening oneself to meeting another with grace and holding space for the possibility of deeper connections to occur, the most painful wounds can begin to heal and light can enter through the cracks of the walls we have built to protect ourselves.

Postscript

Five years after working with Virginia, I received an email from her. She wanted me to know that she was thriving and that ever since our work together, she had managed to stay out of residential treatment. While her experience with bulimia has left a permanent mark in many ways and she still needed to remind herself that support was available, she felt that she had enough internal capacity to keep herself safe. Virginia also let me know that she was now married with a two-year-old son and was pregnant with her second child. She said that she now experiences support from her husband in a way that allows her to feel her own strength in partnership with another. "Arrow and the herd helped me see that I could be clear and ask for support. Like a bow and arrow, both come together with their individual strengths to make something more formidable. I think of Arrow often. We named our son, Beau. If we have a girl next, we might just name her, Reba!"

Case Study 2: Helpers Need Help, Too

A couple of years ago, I was invited to lead an EFP program for people caring for patients diagnosed with stage-four cancer. This particular group comprised six men and women between 36 and 65 years of age, with spouses and partners who were struggling with various stages of their diseases. Some of the patients were already in hospice and palliative care, and others were still living at home.

The awareness of death as an existential given is clearly inescapable when caring for someone who is dying, and grief is not only reserved for the finality of death but is an experience of continuous loss, day by day. The group members were referred to me with a host of co-occurring presenting issues such as anxiety, depression, and insomnia. They had come to this group to find solace from others who were experiencing the same fears and impending reality of losing a loved one. This particular session occurred about four weeks into the twelve-week program I was offering.

All but one group member arrived on time for the start of the session. I had not received a call or text from the missing group member, Todd, so wanted to give him a few minutes' grace before starting in case he was stuck in traffic. I had planned to introduce an activity in which the group would pair up and groom the horses as a way of attending to self-regulation. Aware that with Todd missing, I would have an odd number, I decided to let go of the plan for the time being.

I noticed that the rest of the group was unusually quiet as we waited. I knew that Todd's wife was in hospice care, and he had mentioned the week before that he didn't think that she would hold out for much longer, so I wondered silently if she had passed away. I could feel the group members retreating into their own fears as the unvoiced question hovered around us.

> **Me**: I notice how quiet everyone is right now. What's going on for you?
>
> **Brad:** I can't speak for anyone else, but I'm feeling torn between wanting to spend time with the horses and wanting to go home and check on my wife. I'm worried about Todd. I imagine that him not being here is because it's bad news with his wife. He said she wasn't doing well last week.
>
> **Me:** How do you all feel about waiting for a couple more minutes to see if he gets in touch or shows up?
>
> **Nancy:** Yes, I think I'd like that.
>
> **Wendy:** I don't know. I'm fine to wait, but he's never late, so I feel like we're just waiting for the inevitable.
>
> **Brad:** Maybe, but I'd like to hold on to some hope for now. Let's wait.

I was struck by the poignancy of their responses. I felt a heaviness in my heart as I imagined how hope and inevitability regarding their loved ones were a constant presence for them. I chose not to open that up at that moment and, instead, we waited in silence for a couple of minutes longer. With no word from Todd, I invited the group to head towards the barn. I watched as they walked silently up the driveway, heads drooped and shoulders slumped, without the usual chatter among them. We paused outside the barn, next to the pasture where the horses were grazing, and went through our safety protocol. I was about to invite the group into the pasture when the sound of gunshots interrupted me. While the sound of gunfire was unexpected in that moment, it was also not unusual in my neighborhood for people to hold target practice on their property. This did not mean that my horses had become accustomed to the sound. As the first shot rang out, the horses startled and began to run.

We watched as the herd galloped from one end of the field to the other, with my gelding Arrow leading the way and the mares hot on his tail. They came flying towards the fence in front of us before deftly turning and accelerating away. On the second lap around the field, my mare Reba had taken the lead. Being an ex-reining horse, she came galloping at full speed towards the fence line before executing a perfect sliding stop directly in front of us. Without missing a beat, she turned on her haunches, performing an exquisite spin before launching off across the field once more.

Meanwhile, my other mare, Cheyenne, was trying to keep up. With her arthritis, Cheyenne was less fluid in her movements. I watched as she pulled herself up on her hind legs to spin around and winced as she landed heavily on the ground. I was simultaneously grateful that it had rained heavily recently so the ground offered a softer landing for her and irritated at the sight of the horses churning up the field.

As Arrow came up to the fence line, he slowed to a trot. Breathing heavily and sweating profusely, he turned towards the mares, who were still galloping around, exhaled, and trotted off to rejoin them.

Looking around the group, I saw that the herd had captured their attention. I also realized that, much as I love watching the athleticism of my herd in moments like these, I knew that if Arrow continued trying to keep up with the mares, it would increase his chances of coming up lame. I asked the group to assist me in getting the herd's attention by exhaling audibly with some "horsey breaths" while I stepped into the pasture to ask them to whoa. The horses gradually came to a halt, and I turned my attention back to the group.

> **Me:** What's happening for each of you right now?
> **Wendy:** That was incredible! They're so strong and powerful.
> **Brad:** That was quite the show, wasn't it? The word that came to mind for me was "vitality"
> **Mark:** I feel quite intimidated. I can still feel the adrenalin of it all.
> **Nancy:** I don't know why, but I feel really, really angry. I was really enjoying watching them. They looked so amazing, and then you went in and stopped them. I don't know why you had to cut them short, and I don't know why that made me so angry.
> **Alisha:** I resonate with that, Nancy. I'm not angry though. I'm feeling sad more than anything. I didn't like it that Veronica stopped them either, but I imagine it had something to do with their safety. Is that why? All I know is that it makes me realize even more how I have no idea how or when my wife's life will be cut short, and it will be entirely out of my control.

Usually, when clients ask about horse behaviors, I will gently redirect to enquire as to what that behavior means to them. In this instance, it felt important to acknowledge that I was looking out for Arrow in a preventative way, as it felt relevant to the theme that was beginning to emerge in the group. I shared with them my concern about how running at full speed might aggravate his lameness and acknowledged that my interruption of this had brought up something painful for the group. This opened up a dialogue around how none of us is able to predict the future, and how they each have small choices and some control over how they respond to what's happening for them and their partners as they move through this experience with one another.

> **Nancy:** I'm sorry I got so worked up about that, Veronica.
> **Me:** Absolutely no need to apologize. Whatever is happening for you is valid. Of course, you're angry. You have every right to feel that way about what's happening in your life.
> **Nancy:** I'm just so exhausted, I think it doesn't take much to set me off.

Alisha: I know what you mean. I'm wiped—emotionally and physically. I know that my husband doesn't want a lot of people to see him in his current state, so I feel like I have to take care of him on my own. Other than you guys, I don't think other people understand how exhausting it all is.

Wendy: I totally get that. It's not just the taking care of them that's exhausting. It's pretending that I'm okay that's really taking its toll! I'm so tired I just want to curl up in bed for a week and not get up.

As she said this, I noticed that the horses had meandered across the field to the shade under some trees. We watched as Cheyenne sniffed the ground and dropped to her knees. Groaning, she turned onto her back and massaged her spine into the ground. She flipped onto her side and stretched her legs straight out in front of her and flopped her head onto the ground with an additional groan.

Nancy: Oh my goodness! What's happening? Is she okay? I didn't think that horses lay down like that!

Alisha: Did you hear her groaning? Is that normal? Do we need to go and check if she's okay?

Me: I hear your concern about Cheyenne. We can certainly move closer to her if you'd like to.

As the group approached, we could see that Cheyenne had her eyes closed and was snoring loudly.

Nancy (laughing): Is she snoring? I didn't realize that horses snored!

Wendy: That's so funny. I guess she really did tire herself out earlier.

Meanwhile, Reba had walked over close to Cheyenne, sniffed the ground and dropped to her knees and rolled, flipping from one side to the other and back again. Tucking her legs up underneath her, Reba rested her head on the ground in front of her and closed her eyes.

Brad: Looks like Reba is going for a nap, too.

Mark (pointing to Arrow): Yep, they all are. Arrow's lying down now, too. That's hilarious! It's group nap time.

Wendy: That must be nice to be able to just lie down and take a nap whenever you need.

Nancy: Doesn't have to be a nap. Just stopping to rest would be nice.

Me: How would it be for you all to have a rest right now?

I reminded the group that we had folding chairs available, and if they wanted to bring them into the pasture, we could. Brad and Mark immediately volunteered to go and fetch the chairs from the barn. I invited the group to position themselves somewhere in the pasture where they felt comfortable, as long as they stayed within hearing distance of one another. Taking their chairs, the group members spread themselves out around the sleeping horses. I watched as they sank into the chairs with a sigh.

Me: As you get settled, notice how you're feeling in your body. Pay attention to where you might be holding some tension and breathe into that space. Feel free to close your eyes if that feels good to you. Know that I have an eye on the horses and safety, and if you need to move, I'll let you know.

I watched as each of them began to let go of some tension. I could see that Brad had closed his eyes and was sitting with his back away from the chair, and his hands on his knees, with his head tilted towards the sky. Wendy sat with her eyes closed, upright and supported in her chair, with her hands in her lap. Her legs were stretched out in front of her with her right foot crossed over her left ankle. After a few moments, they both repositioned themselves so that their arms were resting on either side of the armrests, and they could let go of some of the tension in their shoulders. Brad also sat further back so that he was resting his back against the chair.

I encouraged the group to pay attention to their breath, and to listen to the sounds of the horses breathing. Gradually, I saw the softening of Mark's jaw, the lowering of Wendy's hand as she released some tension in her arms, the deepening of Nancy's breath, and felt the general easing into a space of tranquility. This silence felt decidedly different to the one at the beginning of the session. That silence was heavy with unanswered questions. This silence felt restful, and I wanted to give the group as much of it as possible.

I paid attention to the small movements in the horses. The flick of an ear and the slow opening and closing of their eyes. I paid attention to my own breath and took in the sensation of the ground beneath my feet. I watched the group to get a feel for when they had reached their tolerance for the quiet space. After about ten minutes, I walked around and checked in with each of them individually. I wanted to see if they wanted to continue in the quiet space, and I wanted their decision to be based on their own desires rather than a group consensus. Every member of the group wanted more, so we continued for another five minutes with the restful silence.

A hawk circled above us and called to its mate, a loud piercing shriek. Arrow and Reba both lifted their heads. The group members began to stir, opening and rubbing their eyes and stretching out their arms and legs. I invited the group to circle round so that we could process their experiences. As the group members formed their circle, Arrow and Reba stood up, shook themselves down, and wandered over to us. Cheyenne remained lying flat out on the ground, sound asleep.

> **Me:** I see Arrow and Reba have joined us. How are you all feeling after that little group nap?
>
> **Wendy:** That was so relaxing. I like it that these two have joined us now. It's like they've had their nap so now they can pay attention to what's happening.
>
> **Nancy:** I feel calmer and less on edge.
>
> **Brad:** I think I actually nodded off, but I could hear the horses snoring, and that felt so comforting.
>
> **Alisha:** I like how Cheyenne is still fast asleep even though everyone else is up. I feel like she's telling me that it's okay to take care of myself, and I can have some control in my life. It doesn't matter if it's not convenient to other people.
>
> **Wendy:** Yes, and that it's okay not to pretend how you're feeling. It's okay to say I'm exhausted, rather than pretend to be strong in case it's awkward for the other person.
>
> **Brad:** I agree. It's all very well for us to be the ones helping our partners, but we need help, too. I think I need to tell people what I need instead of trying to soldier on by myself.

Arrow stepped into the middle of the circle. Slowly, he pivoted his way around the group and stretched his neck out to sniff each person in turn. Reba had stayed to one side of the circle, but as Arrow stepped into the middle, she positioned herself between Wendy and

Nancy. Bracketing my amusement at my horses' antics, I asked the group what they were taking away from the session.

> **Wendy** (stroking Reba as she talked): That I can't keep pretending that I'm okay, and that I need to take time to rest. Reba is telling me that there's no way I can be there for others if I don't rest myself.
>
> **Nancy** (with Arrow sniffing her face): I'm learning that it's not my job to make others feel less awkward about my pain. If I can tell people I'm hurting, then maybe I'll get some support—even if it's awkward. Arrow clearly has no qualms about being in the middle of us and telling us what he needs. And if he didn't, I wouldn't be getting this amazing muzzle rub!

In wrapping up the session, I shared with the group that what they had articulated reminded me of a poem entitled "You must be strong" by Sophia Diotima. I pulled out my phone to find a copy of it to read to them.

"You Must be Strong"
by Sophia Diotima

"You must be strong."
Why?
Where does it say
In your book of rules
That I "must" be "strong"?
And who are you
To question my strength?
What you wish for me
Is not that I should be strong
But that I would be easy...
Easy to deal with
Non-taxing, not embarrassing
That I should not break your convention
You wish me not strength
But silence
And I will not comply.

As I finished reading, I received a text from Todd. He wanted to apologize to the group for missing the session, and to let them know that he was okay. He knew that we would be worried about his wife. He had simply fallen asleep and had only just woken up and realized that he had missed our session. I relayed the information to the group.

> **Wendy:** Oh, I'm so glad he's okay.
> **Nancy:** Me, too. Sounds like he was one step ahead of us in today's session anyway. I'm glad he got some rest, too.

This case study highlights the many choice points that may arise during a session. I could have jumped in at the beginning with an exploration of what Wendy and Brad felt about inevitability and hope; I could have delved into the group's response to the sound of gunfire; I could have enquired more about the feelings of vitality and power they experienced from the horses; I could have spent more time processing the anger that was elicited by my interrupting the horses' athletic display; or I could have focused on their concern for Cheyenne when she lay down. Each of those avenues would have been interesting and could have taken us to different insights for each person, and yet the theme of self-care and regulation would still be present.

By following the figure that emerged in each moment rather than placing a predetermined agenda on the process, we were able to co-create a meaningful experience with the horses. By letting go of my original plan of working with the horses in a more structured way, I was able to attend to the needs of the clients in the moment. The existential theme of isolation showed up in the group members' struggle to articulate how alone they felt in their everyday lives. Through the experience of attending to self-care, they were able to regain a sense of their own strength without feeling the need to diminish the painful process of grieving while loved ones were still living. The goal of the session was to attend to self-regulation, which is what transpired. All roads lead to Rome.

Case Study 3: Stand by Me

One of my favorite programs to lead is a recurring women's group that was the inspiration for our Daring HERD® retreats. The Daring HERD® curriculum is designed to bring together the HERD model with the work of Brené Brown's Daring Way™. As a Certified Daring Way™ Facilitator, I often combine my knowledge from this modality into what we offer at The HERD Institute®. Brené Brown's work resonates with me deeply. Her research into shame and vulnerability as a universal experience normalizes the pain of those moments and soothes our feelings of existential isolation through an injection of empathy. Her research findings fit beautifully with the HERD approach of working with compassion and authenticity.

This particular group is held as a two-day retreat on a biannual basis and has been running in some form or another for the past five years. The group is held at a stunning equestrian facility that has ample space for break-out sessions, as well as private spots for contemplation. There's a pond with a wooden dock where people can sit and relax, and there are various judges' stands and gazebos for more privacy. The back of the property opens up into numerous pastures where the herd of 30 horses graze on rotation, and to the east of the property are some wooded trails. The owner of the facility, Heather, is a high-level dressage rider who loves introducing her herd to novel experiences. Each time I return to the property, there is a new obstacle in the arena or a newly cut trail through the woods. It's a peaceful and inspiring setting to work in, and I always feel a spark of creativity when I arrive.

Over the years, the group members have changed. What began as a mother and daughter connection workshop has shifted to focusing on women who are in a transitional time of their lives. From new mothers and empty nesters, career women entering retirement and newly relocated professionals to the newly married and recently divorced, the aim is to facilitate a transformative experience in the safety of sisterhood. While we have accepted new members to the group, there have been a core number of women who have attended every session.

This case study outlines one of these sessions during the third year of the group. As always, the group consisted of women from different walks of life, all experiencing major life changes. They were all trying to find their way in a newly defined role or place, looking for others they could connect with, and trying to find a sense of belonging. There were twelve women in the group, aged between 28 and 56, and while a few of them knew one another, many of them were attending the group for the first time. The group members had varying levels of experience with horses, from basic knowledge to competition-level dressage. The barn owner, Heather, subscribed to a holistic approach to horsemanship and was taking part in the session as my equine professional.

I started the day with some herd observation and a theme had begun to emerge among the participants about how difficult it is to feel connected in their busy lives and how scary it feels to reach out for support. Making new friends as an adult is tough, and being in a new area without a support network can be overwhelming. Despite the different life stages and the transitions that the individuals were experiencing, there was a commonality that emerged within the group around how isolated they had been feeling. The risk of taking the first step towards another to initiate friendship is fraught with anxiety and fears of rejection.

During the session, we were working in the outdoor arena with three mares, Sugar, Annabelle, and Daisy. The horses were not new to the barn but they were relatively new to one another and had only been turned out together a few times earlier that week. I had invited the women to form groups of four, and each group had chosen a horse to partner with.

In their groups, one person was holding the lead rope, another was walking along on the horse's off-side, and two people acted as observers. They were practicing leading with purpose as an experience of feeling their intention in an embodied way. Things were going smoothly as the groups led their horses around the arena. Suddenly, Sugar stopped and refused to move. The other two groups slowed to a halt behind her. I noticed that Sugar was trying to turn her head towards the rest of the group. At the same time, I noticed that the other two mares, Daisy and Annabelle, were trying to pull forward towards Sugar, so the women were attempting to keep the horses in line, with one group turning in a circle with Annabelle, and the other backing Daisy up a few steps. There was a lot going on.

I was aware of several figures emerging for me in that moment: Sugar, Annabelle, and Daisy were relatively new to one another, the women were also relatively new to one another, the horses were pulling towards one another, and the women were turning in circles and/or directing the horses away from one another. I considered the choice points that were available to me—namely, whether to pay attention to the novelty of the relationships or focus on what was happening between the horses. I chose the latter.

Me: What are you noticing about the horses right now?
Keisha: I think Sugar wants to be able to see the other two.
Chrissy: I think Daisy's feeling anxious.

Barbara: I think they're all feeling a bit antsy.

Me: I see that the group with Annabelle asked her to turn in a circle, and the group with Daisy asked her to back up a few steps. What's happening for you now?

Lorraine: I'm sure that Annabelle's feeling frustrated about going around in circles. I know that's how I feel about my life sometimes. Being pulled into doing the same things and hoping for different results. Isn't that the definition of crazy?

Keisha: I'm relating to that, too. Plus, if you add in Daisy backing up, that's pretty much my life—one step forward and two steps back, and then I'm turning in circles—girlfriend, I may as well be square dancing! No wonder I don't feel like I belong. Take this big mama to a hoedown and see how I stand out!

The women laughed as Keisha danced a few steps in a square formation and twirled around. I resonated deeply with her feeling of difference, and as the only other person of color in the arena, I felt an affinity towards her.

Me: I hear you, Keisha. I also notice you making a joke about something that feels important, about not belonging.

Keisha: I did, I did...but y'all know how it's so much easier to joke around than to feel the pain, right?

Lorraine: Totally. I feel that pain too, though. Not belonging.

Me: I'd like to pay more attention to what's coming up for you all, and I'm aware that Daisy and Annabelle are still moving around. How might we support them with what they might need right now?

Chrissy: Why don't we let them off lead and see what they do?

This suggestion was met with several nods around the group. I reminded the group to watch out for safety while the horses were at liberty before asking them to let the horses off lead. Once free, the horses all walked to the middle of the arena. They stood facing the center and one another, and began to exhale. One by one, they blew out some big breaths, and stepped in closer to one another. I asked the group what they thought was happening.

Chrissy: They just wanted to be together.
Keisha: They were all being led in different directions, so now they're reconnecting.
Lorraine: They're just hanging out with their friends.
Me: I'm hearing a similar theme from earlier, about making friends. What's it like for you to see them standing together like this?

I looked around the group of women and saw that several of them had become tearful. Wiping the tears from her eyes, one woman started talking about how hard it was for her to see how bonded the horses were, as she had recently relocated to the area and was now living across the country from her two sisters. She missed them deeply and was feeling homesick. This resonated for others in the group who were missing children who had left for college and opened up a discussion on grief and loss for humans and animals that were no longer with us. Each woman began to share her story of yearning for connection, missed opportunities, and/or her fear of rejection.

I noticed that during this discussion, the horses had remained together in the middle of the arena. We were standing in a circle at one end of the arena. I was curious about the type of connection that the women might want with the horses, and how they might reach for that.

Me: I'm hearing a lot from all of you about missing or wanting connection. I see that the horses are still standing in the middle of the arena facing one another, while we are all at this end of the arena. What do you make of that?
Tina: I'd like to interact with them more, but I don't want to disturb them.
Keisha: I want them to notice us. I want them to want to be with us.
Barbara: It's weird, but I feel like I'm back in high school again. Like they're all whispering about us or something.
Chrissy: Haha! That's funny. I was just talking to someone the other day about how that happens when I take the kids to school. Like, not only are my kids the new kids on the block, but so am I, and everyone's all cliquey in their groups already, and I have to figure out which group I want to join.

Lorraine: Yes, and once you decide which one, whether they'll let you join, right?

The women nodded their agreement. The yearning for connection was becoming more apparent. I wanted the group to experience some connection between the horses and one another. The aim of the activity of intentionally leading the horses had gone awry, so I was wondering how to redirect them. It struck me then that I was in a catch-22: Pushing my agenda of having them lead with intention would negate their ability to find their own intention. My leading them towards something would not support their process of discovering how they could reach for something they desired. I needed to wait it out and allow them to feel the support that was available, but not do it for them. Looking at the horses, I noticed the story forming in my mind was that they were waiting for the women to initiate something too.

Me: So, I notice how we're talking about the "what if" scenarios outside of this space with one another. I'm wondering how all that applies right now with us and the horses.

Tina: It feels really vulnerable to ask people if they want to be your friend, or to say that you need help.

Keisha: Yes, it does. It takes a lot of courage to make the first step.

Me: As Brené Brown says, there's no courage without vulnerability, right?

Chrissy: Yes! But it's only possible to be brave when we have support.

Me: What support do you have or need right now?

Lorraine: I think it really helps to know that we are all wanting the same thing. That makes me feel less alone and more connected. We all just want to feel like we belong.

Barbara: Just like the horses.

Me: How might this relate to what's happening right now between us and the horses?

Tina: I think they're waiting for us to make the first move.

Keisha turned to the horses, cupped her hands around her mouth, and called out to the mares, "Hey ponies! Wanna be our friends?" she asked. The women giggled. Keisha looked around the group, "That wasn't as scary as I thought it would be. Maybe we could all try it and see if they respond?" The women began calling out to the horses. They called their names in sing-song voices. They repeated Keisha's question. They asked if they wanted to come and play.

The horses pricked up their ears. Daisy turned away from the herd to face the group. Sugar took a couple of steps towards us. Annabelle followed. Slowly, the horses began to walk in our direction. Checking in with the group, I saw that they expressed joy, excitement, validation, gratitude, surprise, and hope that the horses had responded to their calls. As the horses approached, I invited the women to connect with the horses in whatever way they chose. A few people stepped forward towards the mares. The rest of the group dispersed around the arena to give the horses more space.

Sugar led the way and walked towards Chrissy, who had been leading her in the initial activity. Chrissy stepped forward to meet Sugar, reaching up to stroke her face, before turning and walking alongside her. Sugar followed. Chrissy walked over to Keisha, who had also been in her group previously, and Keisha joined in to walk with Chrissy and Sugar. They continued walking around the arena, with Sugar walking between them. Each time they approached a group member, they asked if they'd like to join in. Soon, Sugar was walking along at liberty with half of the group spaced out around her.

Meanwhile, Daisy and Annabelle had approached Barbara. The eldest member of the group, Barbara was limited in her mobility, and walked with a cane. By this point in the process, she had opted to use the folding stool that formed part of her cane and was perched on it near the arena gate. Daisy and Annabelle had positioned themselves in front of Barbara, facing her. The rest of the group was spread out around the two mares. A couple of them were petting the horses as they watched the others walking with Sugar. After a few minutes, the group stopped walking, and I checked in with everyone.

Me: What's happening right now?
Lorraine: That was awesome! I loved that Sugar decided to walk with us.
Me: You stepped up and made the first move. How was that for you?
Lorraine: It felt good. She was like, yeah, I'll be your friend. It wasn't as scary as I thought it would be. But I wasn't the

first one to make the move, Keisha did when she started calling out to all of them.

Me: That's right. Keisha. What's it like for you to see the impact of what you started?

Keisha: It's amazing! Who knew this would happen? Honestly, I was kinda just messing around when I called out to them. I didn't think that they'd respond. Heather, you've got these horses well trained. Hahaha!

Heather: Haha! I'm not sure I could train them to do that even if I tried. That was all you.

This led to a discussion on how often each woman had experienced something successful, only to diminish or dismiss their own part in it. One woman commented on how easy it was for her to praise and encourage others in their achievements, but so much harder for her to acknowledge her own accomplishments. Another commented on how she preferred to be part of a group sometimes so that she didn't stand out, whether it was for something good or bad.

Keisha: I sing in my church choir. I totally get the not wanting to stand out thing. I've been asked to sing solos and lead the congregation, but I'm not sure I'm brave enough. I want to, because I truly believe that singing is the best form of prayer—or at least, how I like to pray—but the idea of leading terrifies me.

Lorraine: Oh, I'd love to hear you sing!

Tina: Me, too!

Chrissy: I heard you singing to yourself this morning. You have a beautiful voice. I'd love to hear you sing more.

Me: It sounds like you have an audience right here, Keisha. How does that feel?

Keisha (laughing): Terrifying! But in a good way, I guess.

I asked the group how we might incorporate the different aspects that had emerged during the session so far into an experience with the horses. The themes of taking risks, feeling supported, being met by the horses, and feeling a sense of unity were all part of the mix. After a few moments of discussion, the group came up with a plan.

Chrissy: We've nominated Keisha to lead us in a song. Those of us who want to sing, can. But no one has to do anything they don't want to do.

Keisha: I'm okay with that, as long as someone else joins in

Tina: I will. I think we should sing while we walk around and see if the horses will walk with us.

Lorraine: Maybe those of us who don't want to sing can keep time or something?

Heather: We have some barrels you can use as drums. And there are some hula-hoops that rattle. You could use those as maracas. The horses are all familiar with those. Barbara, if you'd like to sit on the mounting block instead of your stool, I can bring that over for you.

Barbara: Yes, that would be great. Thank you.

With their plan in place, the group gathered their "instruments" and prepared to sing. The horses had meandered around the arena sniffing at barrels and hula-hoops as they appeared.

Keisha counted the group in, "5, 6, 7, 8....In the jungle, the mighty jungle, the lion sleeps tonight," she began to sing. Her voice rang out clearly across the arena, and a breeze blew. I looked up and saw birds flying by, took a deep breath, and exhaled. The horses' ears swiveled, and they half turned their heads towards Keisha. Chrissy was standing near Sugar. Stroking her neck, Chrissy walked a few paces forward and joined in with the song. Sugar turned her head back towards Chrissy and walked towards her.

Barbara walked over to the mounting block that Heather had carried across the arena. As she sat down, she bumped the heel of her foot against the side of the mounting block, causing a loud thump. It was a deep, reverberating sound. The horses turned towards her, and Barbara thumped the block again. Sugar continued walking behind Chrissy, and a few other women joined the procession, with Daisy and Annabelle walking along with them. Barbara continued to thump out a bass rhythm with the mounting block, while Lorraine and Tina kept in time with their barrel drums. A couple of others had taken up the hula-hoops and began rattling them, slightly off beat. The sound was jarring against Keisha's voice, and didn't fit with the rest of the group.

Keisha trailed off mid verse, and the drumming and rattling stopped. Everyone stood still, horses and humans. I asked the group what was happening.

Keisha: I thought more people would join in with the singing, and I started to feel shy so I stopped.
Lorraine: It was hard to keep time to.
Tina: Yes, I wanted to join in with singing but didn't know the words.
Chrissy: The hula-hoops didn't really do much for the song either. Maybe we can sing something a little slower? Would you be willing to lead us again Keisha?

Keisha nodded, took a breath and began to sing, "When the night has come, and the land is dark, and the moon is the only light we see..." The women cheered, and began to join in. Barrels, hula-hoops, and mounting block bass. Thump, thump, thump. The horses followed the women around the arena as they sang. I felt my eyes tear up at the sight of these courageous women, finding joy in connection with one another and the horses. Keisha and Chrissy, were leading the singing and walking, changing directions as the horses followed, and linking arms as they went. Tina and Lorraine keeping time with their instruments, were smiling brightly and singing along. Everyone was part of the process in some way, and my heart filled with joy.

This experience marked the beginning of the sisterhood that these women co-created with one another over the rest of the retreat. Throughout the weekend, we returned to the themes of vulnerability and courage, isolation and belonging, and the joy of being part of a supportive collective. I felt honored to have been a part of their process and inspired by their courage and resilience.

This case study highlights, once again, how holding a loose framework of the existential themes that a client population may bring can allow for a more fluid approach to holding space in a session. Letting go of my agenda and plan enabled these women to empower themselves in a way that would not have been possible otherwise. It also demonstrates how important it is for the therapist to be aware of their own process in each moment in order to not impose their own agenda onto their clients' experience. It calls for us to continuously look for our blind spots and biases and be open to differences in culture and how these differences show up in our work.

Case Study 4: Attunement for Support[*]

Ben and Marie were referred to me for couple's therapy through a family therapy service. The agency had been working in a family setting with them and their 14-year-old daughter. Their family therapist felt that it would be beneficial for them to attend a series of EFP sessions with me to focus on their partnership. Marie had recently revealed to the family therapist via email that she had experienced some childhood sexual trauma that she was reluctant to talk about during family therapy.

In the assessment process, Ben voiced frustration that he felt isolated in the family process. He explained that however much he tried to engage in family matters, Marie would sidestep his attempts to become involved. Marie explained that each time Ben tried to intervene, she would feel criticized in how she was handling the situation with their daughter. They both agreed that they needed some help to reconnect with each other. Their presenting issue in family therapy was their teenage daughter's struggle with bulimia nervosa. Ben and Marie recognized how their daughter's illness had impacted on the relationships within the family but were also aware that the ruptures were not all because of her illness. Ben had also recently been made aware of Marie's trauma history but did not know the details.

After going through the HERD safety protocol, I invited Ben and Marie to enter the paddock to meet and greet the horses. It was a bright, sunny day, and the horses were peacefully grazing in the paddock. They were standing close together near one corner of the field, with their backs to us as we entered. As the couple approached, one of the mares swiveled an ear towards them, picked up her head, and trotted towards the opposite side of the field. She was quickly followed by her two herd members. Once there, they dropped their heads and resumed their grazing. Ben and Marie stopped in their tracks and turned towards the herd once more. Again, they began their approach. Once more, the mare swiveled her ear, picked up her head, and trotted away. The other two horses followed. The couple stopped and turned towards the herd. I asked them to describe their

---

[*] This case study was originally published in A Horse is a Horse, of Course: 1st International Symposium for Equine Welfare and Wellness (*Parent*, 2017). It has been edited and republished here with additional notes.

experience so far. Ben said that he was feeling disappointed that the horses didn't want to engage with him. Marie said that she felt they didn't want to be disturbed and wanted to wait to see if they would come to her.

> **Me:** How do these feelings show up in your relationship?
> **Ben:** Oh, all the time. I'm constantly feeling like she doesn't want anything to do with me.
> **Marie:** That's not true! Of course, I want you to be involved. I just don't know how to let you in.

Marie's shoulders slumped, and she looked down at the ground and became tearful. "I know it's not fair on you. I just don't know how to let go," she said. "I wish you'd let me help," said Ben.

This interaction created some palpable tension between them, and I noticed the horses had moved further away. Wanting the couple to explore how they shared space with each other, I invited them to take a few moments and observe the herd and to choose a horse that they would like to work with together. After a brief discussion, they pointed to Reba, the chestnut mare who had led the others to walk away. Reminding them to pay attention to the themes of inclusion and letting go, I asked them to go and spend some time with Reba.

As the couple approached her, Reba picked her head up from grazing and stood with her ears pointing towards them and remained in place. Marie stopped about 10 feet away from her, while Ben continued to walk right up to Reba's side. Reba shifted her weight away from Ben but continued to stand in place. As Ben reached up to stroke her face, Reba took a few steps sideways away from him and turned her head away. I was paying close attention to Reba's responses, knowing that she does not like it when strangers stroke her face. I was prepared to intervene if he continued.

Meanwhile, Marie had been approached by the other mare in the herd, Cheyenne, who had started nudging her on the arm with her muzzle. As Reba continued to sidestep away from Ben, Marie began to sidestep away from Cheyenne, moving closer to Ben.

> **Me:** I noticed that Reba stood with you until you reached up to stroke her face.
> **Ben:** Yes, she did. I thought because she was staying with me I could ask her for more.

Me: What would it be like for you to focus on being with her at a level that she is comfortable with?
Ben: I don't know. I'm not sure I would be able to tell what she's comfortable with. I guess I was focusing on what I wanted from her.
Marie: I would think that if she moved away, it would be a good indication that it was too much.

At this, I turned to Marie.

Me: What's happening for you right now?
Marie: Well...the horses seem to have cornered us, and I'm feeling a little overwhelmed.
Me: Where would you feel more comfortable?
Marie (taking a few steps away from the horses and Ben): This is better.

I asked if they would be willing to explore their sense of boundaries with a game involving hula-hoops. Retrieving the hula-hoops from outside the paddock where I had placed them earlier, I gave one to each of them. Immediately, Marie put the hula-hoop around her waist and held onto it like a swim ring. Ben held onto his at arms' length and twirled it in his hands. I asked them to approach the herd together with the hula-hoops, paying attention to how the horses responded to them, and to what emotions and sensations they might notice in themselves. Ben began by approaching Reba, holding out the hula-hoop for her to sniff. Reba stretched out her neck towards him and grabbed the hula-hoop with her teeth. They proceeded to play a game of tug before they both let go. Ben laughed and picked up the hoop and continued the game with Reba.

Meanwhile, Marie had approached Cheyenne, still with the hula-hoop around herself. Cheyenne backed away from her a few steps, and Marie stopped. She stood for a while with the hula-hoop around her, watching Cheyenne. After a while, she dropped the hula-hoop onto the ground, still standing inside the hoop, looked around and watched Ben playing with Reba. Cheyenne took a few steps towards her but stayed just out of reach. Marie took a step forward, still inside the hoop, and reached out to stroke Cheyenne, who responded by lifting her neck up and closing her eyes. Marie proceeded to scratch Cheyenne's neck.

Watching this unfold, I was acutely aware of my own responses. I was surprised that Reba had responded to Ben with her tug-of-war, as she was usually terrified of the hula-hoop. I was equally surprised by Cheyenne's reactions as she was usually unfazed by any arena props. Having worked in a therapeutic riding environment, Cheyenne was accustomed to a wide range of scenarios, toys, and sensations. The contrast between their habitual behaviors and what was happening in the moment with the two mares intrigued me. I put these thoughts aside and focused on the process unfolding before me. I asked Ben and Marie to describe what they were experiencing in the moment.

Marie expressed delight in her contact with Cheyenne, experiencing her as being respectful of her boundaries while they got to know each other. She felt safe inside her hula-hoop. Ben said he had enjoyed his game with Reba, but also realized that he had been playing a tug-of-war of sorts with Marie, which wasn't so enjoyable. In his desire to support her through her trauma, he hadn't considered how invasive it was for Marie.

> **Ben:** It's like I want to be inside your hoop with you. But I can see that's too much for you now.
>
> **Marie:** Yes, that would be too overwhelming for me, and doesn't give me space to breathe.

As we talked, Reba walked towards us and stood between Ben and Marie. Cheyenne walked away and resumed grazing. Marie expressed disappointment that Cheyenne had left, as she was hoping that she would want some more attention from her. "This is what confuses me!" said Ben. "When you get attention, you don't want it. When the attention isn't there, that's when you crave it. Cheyenne was giving you attention earlier and you backed away, but now that she walks away, you want her back. And Reba's right here, but you haven't noticed. It's like whenever I show that I'm there for you, you don't acknowledge it and focus on what's missing instead. I wish it wasn't so complicated."

We spent a few minutes processing the meaning that Ben had made of their interactions with the horses, with Marie acknowledging that she found it difficult to take in support when it was available, while simultaneously yearning for it. For Ben, witnessing Marie's struggle with taking in support and connection allowed him to gain a better understanding of the process between them. His own tug-of-war with the hula-hoop with Reba signified his responses to Marie's ambivalent attachment process.

Reba had stayed by their side throughout the conversation. I invited the couple to experiment with playing with Reba together to find a way to connect with each other. Standing in front of Reba, Ben picked up the hula-hoop and held it vertically towards Marie. She responded by holding the other side of the hoop. Together, they approached Reba. I held my breath, convinced that Reba would run away from the hoop. Instead, she dipped her head and stuck her head through the hoop so that it lay on her neck. Ben and Marie were now on either side of Reba. They turned to face forwards. Still holding onto the hoop, with Reba between them, they began to walk around the paddock. When they had completed one loop around the paddock, I asked them to stop and check in with what they were experiencing. Once they stopped, I asked them to remove the hula-hoop from Reba. They did, and she stayed standing between them.

> **Ben:** I feel like I have a better sense of how to respect Marie's space.
> **Marie:** I liked being able to feel your presence, but not feel overwhelmed. Really though, I can't believe Reba let us do that with her!

I shared with them my surprise at Reba's response, and how she habitually shies away from any of the arena props. Marie began to cry.

> **Marie:** I feel like for her to trust us with the hula-hoop must've gone against all her instincts. I feel honored that she chose to do that. Makes me realize it might be possible to let Ben in and take that risk.

This session marked the beginning of Ben and Marie's journey towards understanding how to connect with each other by attuning to the other's availability for contact in each moment. In subsequent sessions, we worked on identifying more clearly Marie's ambivalent attachment process, in contrast to Ben's need for closeness within the relationship. Reba was a constant companion on their journey, offering herself willingly to work with them in each session.

This case study demonstrates the different stages of the HERD approach. From the beginning moments of negotiating how to share space with the herd and each other, Ben and Marie were supported to gain a clearer sense of what they needed individually, and collectively. This allowed them to move into a space where they could release and expand—release from their long-held restrictions and rigidity, and opening up to an expanded way of relating to each other. This was further deepened by the activity with the hula-hoops with the horses before coming to a place where they felt more at home in themselves and in the relationship. They were able to then reflect on the process and integrate their experience in a way that had meaning for them in their everyday lives.

This case study also highlights the importance of trusting the herd's ability to self-regulate. While Ben and Marie were moving through the five stages, the herd was also doing this. Working at liberty, they are given the choice to participate in sessions, or not. At each moment, they have the freedom to disengage with the process if they so wish. This session demonstrated the importance of allowing the horses to volunteer in this way rather than the practitioner assuming a set of responses from the horses. Reba's willingness to facilitate Ben and Marie's connection through overcoming her fear of the hula-hoop became part of the process.

Later on in the journey, we returned to reflect on this first session of how Reba had interacted with them and the hoop. Marie was able to link that to her own process of overcoming her fear of confiding in Ben more about her trauma history. Attending to the horses' needs and allowing time before and after each session for the herd to recalibrate and release is critical. It is imperative that the practitioner is familiar with the horses involved in the session in order to track their habitual ways of releasing tension from the work.

At the end of every client session, Reba will roll, snort, and run around the paddock for a couple of minutes before settling back down to graze. Cheyenne, on the other hand, releases by rolling and then lying down for a nap. Consistent with the philosophical and theoretical roots of the HERD approach, the herd's welfare becomes part of the relational process.

While I was able to follow the activity that I had in mind for the session, my aim for the use of the hula-hoops was held loosely. Other than having a framework of the hula-hoops to represent boundaries, I was not invested in how Ben and Marie wanted to incorporate them. Each of the interactions emerged organically between them and the horses. The tug-of-war and the subsequent walking with the hoop around Reba's neck were both co-created by Ben and Marie with consent from Reba. The session would have turned out very differently if I had placed expectations for them in how to incorporate the hula-hoops. I also did not make explicit the metaphor of the hula-hoops as representations of their boundaries. By allowing them to navigate the hula-hoops themselves, they were able to sink into an embodied experience of their boundaries, which we then explored in their interactions. If I had asked them to use the hula-hoops in a specific way, we may not have reached the same level of insight in each moment. The hula-hoop would have become a task or performance, and the focus of the session. By focusing on the process as it emerged, Ben and Marie were able to see more clearly how their own boundaries impacted their relationship.

It's not about the activity. It's all about relationships!

Case Study 5: She Sees Me

Troy was referred to me by a colleague who worked at the local VA hospital. He had been discharged from the army after an injury involving an IED explosion while deployed in Afghanistan. He had been in rehabilitation for several months and was doing well physically. He still walked with a slight limp from his hip reconstruction, although given the extent of his injuries, he was grateful to be walking at all. After attending a number of traditional therapy group sessions that my colleague was running, Troy decided that it wasn't for him but had agreed to try EFP as an alternative treatment modality.

I had been working with Troy for about three months at the time of this session, and he had developed a bond with my mare Cheyenne. At the beginning of each session, Cheyenne would trot over to the fence and greet him with a whinny. I had been surprised by how attentive Cheyenne had been and the consistency in the manner with which she greeted him each time. I had discussed with Troy the possibility of introducing some mounted work in the previous week, and he had arrived eager to explore what that might look and feel like.

Troy led Cheyenne into the barn to groom her. He patiently and meticulously brushed her body, mane, and tail, and picked her feet. He had grown up with horses on his family farm and was familiar with this routine. Having competed as a child in barrel racing competitions at local events, he had been rediscovering his love of horses since working with me. He had started to volunteer at a local therapeutic riding facility and was even considering training to become an instructor. Troy reported that he was drinking less and engaging more with his friends and family, and that he finally felt like life was beginning to turn a corner for him.

I watched as Troy carefully set Cheyenne's left front hoof back on the ground after cleaning it. She had turned her head to sniff Troy's back and was now nibbling at his shirt. Smiling, he pushed her off and gave her a scratch on her neck. "Silly girl," he said, "always so curious." He walked around to the other side and bent down to pick up her right hoof. Again, she turned and nibbled his shirt. He laughed as he continued to clean her hoof. Straightening up, he reached his arms around her neck and gave her a hug. It warmed my heart to witness their connection, and I smiled at Troy as he gathered up the grooming tools and put them to one side.

> **Troy:** Okay! We're ready. Let's do this.
> **Me:** Great! Let's lead her into the arena then.

We walked in silence into the arena and positioned Cheyenne next to the mounting block. I had explained to Troy that we would be using a bareback pad on Cheyenne, warning him that she was shedding at the time, so it was likely that he would get quite a bit of horse hair on him. I noticed that he was standing by the mounting block pulling pieces of her grey hair off his top.

> **Me:** What's happening for you right now?
> **Troy** (laughing): I know you prepared me for getting covered in her hair, but I didn't realize she would be shedding quite so much!
> **Me:** What does that mean for you?
> **Troy:** Well, I like to know what I'm getting myself into, and I don't like surprises.
> **Me:** What about what we're about to do with Cheyenne? What are you getting into?
> **Troy:** Well, I'm hoping that it will be fun and remind me that I can let go a little, instead of constantly trying to control everything in my life.
> **Me:** Sounds like we can look for some balance in there.
> **Troy:** Absolutely. It's hard trying to live life wanting everything to be black or white. Grey is important too—isn't

it, Cheyenne? Maybe that's why this grey mare has come into my life, to remind me that I need to focus on the grey.

I was aware that Troy's process in recovering from trauma was always present. His need to predict the outcome of everything had been a theme in our work. I was also aware that we were working with horses, and that there is always an inherent risk for clients in that process. It's why we have liability forms, wear helmets, and attend to safety protocols.

I reminded Troy of that now. He nodded solemnly and said that he understood the physical risks that he was taking, acknowledging that it was the emotional risks that were harder for him to deal with. As we talked, Cheyenne turned and nudged Troy on his arm. "I think she's telling me that it's okay and that's she's going to take care of me." He laughed. I encouraged him to take few deep breaths before stepping up onto the mounting block. Handing me the lead rope, he positioned himself on the top step and prepared to mount. Slowly, he swung his leg over Cheyenne and sat down. Cheyenne stood still underneath him.

> **Me:** How do you feel now that you're on her?
> **Troy**: I feel safe. I can feel how rock solid she is under me.
> **Me:** Take a few moments and just breathe with her.
> **Troy:** I don't know why I feel so emotional right now
> **Me:** I see she's still standing still. What are you noticing in your body?
> **Troy:** I feel like it's the first time in a long time that I can relax.

Troy leaned forward and stroked Cheyenne on her neck, telling her what a good girl she was being and thanking her for taking care of him. I asked if he wanted to lean forward to give her a hug, and he nodded. Shifting his weight forward slightly, he leaned down and lay on her neck, draping his arms around her in a hug. Cheyenne remained standing still but dropped her head slightly. Troy began to cry. He buried his face in her neck and hugged her tightly. After a few moments, he slowly sat up and wiped the tears from his face.

> **Troy:** I don't even know why I'm crying. I'm being so stupid. It's not like I've not been on a horse before.
> **Me:** What are you aware of right now?

Troy: Cheyenne hasn't moved at all. This whole time. I'm not sure how comfortable it is for her with me draping myself on her neck, so I sat up. She seems okay, but I'm not sure.

Me: What about you? Was it comfortable for you?

Troy: Well, no. But I was more worried about her.

Me: I appreciate how compassionate you are of her. I'm wondering how we can bring some of that compassion to how you relate to yourself.

Troy (sighing): I know I can be hard on myself. I'm not sure there are many people in my life that I can be this open with. I think if I told my friends and family how I'm really feeling half the time, they'd run a mile. Cheyenne just seems to see right through me.

Me: And how does she respond to what she sees?

Troy (begins to cry again): She just accepts me as I am and stays. She comes to greet me at the gate every time, like she's happy to see me.

Me: How is she responding to you now?

Cheyenne had turned her head towards Troy.

Troy: Either she's wondering what I'm doing on her, or she's telling me that she's okay with how I am

Me: So, what are you doing on her?

Troy: Asking for support, I guess. I'd like to lean forward and give her another hug. Is that okay?

Me: How might you ask her that?

Troy: I guess I could do it slowly and see if she moves. If not, I can take it as consent?

I nodded. Keeping Cheyenne on a loose lead and watching her for signs of discomfort, I watched as Troy slowly leaned forward, talking to Cheyenne as he did so, asking her to let him know if what he was doing was too much for her. He lay down and buried his face in her neck once more. Cheyenne turned slowly. From where I stood, I could see that Troy had lifted his face and was looking directly into her left eye. "She sees me, and I'm okay" he said.

This case study demonstrates the relational process of introducing a mounted experience into an EFP session. Through developing a relationship between the client and horse prior to any mounted work, we can support our clients to feel the embodied connection that our equine partners offer. By paying attention to the subtle shifts in our horse's responses during a mounted session, the client can experience an authentic connection that is not about using the horse as a tool or prop in the process. If Cheyenne had exhibited any signs of discomfort, we would have ended the mounted experience, and that would have brought up other avenues of exploration for Troy. His ability to self-regulate through his tears with support from Cheyenne was a critical part of his recovery from his trauma. We returned to this theme throughout the rest of this time in therapy with me. The attachment that he had developed with Cheyenne helped to support his ability to reach out to others in his life, allowing him to soften and show his vulnerability in a way that he was not able to previously. Troy's journey exemplifies the power of being fully seen by another without the expectation to be anything other than who he was in that moment. Our job as therapists within an EFP setting is to hold the space for those connections to emerge between our clients and horses so that healing can occur within the relationship.

It's not about the activity. It's all about relationships!

EFP Case Studies: Conclusion

These case studies exemplify the HERD EFP Model through the continuous attention to the moment-by-moment unfolding of the relational dynamics between horses and clients. In reality, each of these case studies involved many more details that were not included. Each figure that emerged in sessions was set against the background of the fabric of the clients' lives. Allowing for freedom in the direction of the session, and staying in the here and now, supported the figures to emerge. Once attended to, like waves on a shore, they receded into the background in order for new ones to surface. Each response from the clients opened up different possibilities that could have been explored. The choices made in each moment during a session are as much an intuitive and embodied process as it is a cognitive one.

The philosophical foundations of the HERD model are evident in each case study. Working from a phenomenological approach and paying attention to the I–Thou moments in the here and now, each case study also provides examples of the different stages of the HERD EFP Model of sharing space, release and expand, deepening, coming home to relationships, and integration. The commitment to working within a flexible framework allows us to flow creatively and meet our clients where they need us most. In those moments of being seen and acknowledged, we can support our clients' sense of authentically engaging in relationships. Raising our clients' awareness of how they enter into relationship with the horses, provides insight into how they interact in other relationships in their everyday lives.

In recounting these case studies, I am struck by the depth of feeling I hold for all the clients and horses I have worked with over the years. While not every session runs smoothly, I have been gifted with a deeper understanding of the power of this way of working in every single session. In holding space for my clients and horses, I also recognize that I am holding space for myself. For that, I am truly grateful to have experienced being in relationship with all of them.

Chapter 14

Final Words

In the four years since I wrote my first book, I have come to realize how much I still have to learn. My herd, and all the horses I have partnered with, continuously teach me how to live with compassion, grace, humility, and integrity. In creating The HERD Institute®, I have been privileged to follow my dreams and work in a field that I am passionate to be a part of. The last four years have been hugely rewarding, challenging, and transformative, and I am eager to see what the future brings. As I write, we are preparing for the first HERD Conference in July 2020, where 25 presenters from all over the world will be sharing their expertise and experiences. We are also working hard to build our non-profit Share in the HERD, which aims to offer grants and scholarships for program development, certification, and research. This is part of my commitment to increasing accessibility and diversity within our field. I am excited to see how this will shift our landscape as an industry.

In all of these developments, through all of these changes, I am constantly being pulled in different directions, all while attempting to find some balance in my life. With so many exciting developments on the horizon, I am recognizing the need to pace myself so that I don't fall into my habitual trap of running as fast as I can without attending to some self-care. My aching body and exhausted brain are reminders that it is impossible to go it alone, and I am immensely grateful for the team that I have gathered around me, without whom I would drown in my attempts to keep going. In all this, I feel called to reevaluate how I want to live my life. The new decade opens up infinite possibilities, and as I reflect on the changes from the past few years, I want to step into this liminal space with intention.

Working with horses has taught me not only to be mindful of how I step into relationship with others, but also how I relate to myself and how I make decisions. When working with 1200-pound animals, it's imperative that we pay attention to the subtle nuances in our relational dance with them. Whether I am working with my horses on the ground or in the saddle, I've learned to ask myself four key questions in order to help me decide what my next steps might be. I've also learned that these questions are applicable to any decision I might make in life in general.

1. Is what I am about to do driven by my ego?
2. Is my decision based on what others expect of me?
3. How does this decision fit with my values?
4. How does this decision fit with my mission or vision?

In learning to work with horses, many of us have been taught that we can't let our horses "win" and that we need to show them who's boss. The result is that we end up in a power struggle, feeling like we have to "win" and not back down. For me, that's an ego-driven way of working. I know when my ego is in the driver's seat when I become defensive about a direction that I'm taking. Focusing on "winning" and task completion rather than on the relationship that I'm building is an ego-driven process.

Looking at business opportunities that arise, I'm called to consider whether expanding the business is coming from a place of competitiveness or a genuine desire to offer additional services. In leading an organization, I want to make sure that the decisions I make are reflective of how I want to live my life and not simply a means to an end. I know that my ego can easily succumb to flattery: invitations to present at conferences, contributions to articles, books, and other publications might be interesting and raise my profile, but I need to balance that with my awareness that I don't need to (or want to) conquer the world. So, I can be intentional where I spend my time and energy.

This leads me to my second question: Is my decision based on what others expect of me? My experience with horses has shown me the wide-ranging expectations of this industry and how many people continue to operate from a "horses as commodity and tool" approach rather than from a relational stance. I now know that this is not the approach that I want to take, but this also means not living up to expectations others had of me.

Within a business setting, my unending curiosity leads me on exciting adventures that may not be directly relevant to my work. I get involved in projects, committees, and organizations with enthusiasm. This sometimes results in my taking on far more than I have the capacity for, and yet I'm often tempted to continue for fear of disappointing others. When I step back from making decisions based on others' expectations, I can regroup and become clearer about my boundaries and turn my attention to things that I feel truly called to do.

My third question helps me to figure out what that is. By asking myself how a decision fits with my values, I can bring more attention to the areas of my life and relationships that I want to cultivate and cherish. When working with my horses over the years, I've wrestled with the conflict of applying a technique or method that feels incongruent to who I am and how I want to relate with my equine partner. I realized that I needed to find a way to be with my horses that was consistent with who I am and how I relate to others.

My personal values and my organizational values also need to be aligned. As a trainer who espouses the importance of integrity, compassion, and authenticity, if I don't walk within those values on a personal level, those inconsistencies will show up in my organization, and vice versa. As Brené Brown says, conflict in our lives shows up when we have conflict in our values.

Finally, the question about how my decision fits with my mission or vision emerges from finding clarity in our values. My aim with my horses was never to enter into the show ring in any capacity. Like all of us in the equine-facilitated world, I found solace, comfort, and joy in simply being with the horses. Riding is fun, and while I enjoy the connection I have with my horses in the saddle, it does not define my relationship with each member of my herd. My aim for my horses is for them to live in a healthy environment where they have choice to interact with the human beings I introduce to them. If they are willing to partner with me under saddle, then that's a bonus. My horses have taught me that being intentional in how I relate to them allows for more consistency. Holding my values of compassion and integrity within our relationships also allows me to model that consistency with my students and clients.

From an organizational perspective, The HERD Institute® mission and vision is clearly stated on our website and in our student handbooks. We aim to offer an inclusive environment, embrace an attitude of abundance, and honor the potential of all our members. We want to support our members to develop the integrity of their personal philosophy, expand their knowledge and skills, and broaden their horizons through continuous learning and practice. In this way, we can collectively hold our vision to create a global community of equine-facilitated psychotherapy and learning practitioners who are committed to furthering the work of the pioneers in our field.

Asking myself these four questions reconfirms my desire to uphold our mission and vision. I am thankful for the support of my peers and colleagues as we continue our collaborative efforts towards achieving our shared vision for this industry. I am humbled by how much my students and clients have taught me and feel privileged to have walked with them in their journeys. Above all, I am grateful beyond measure for the compassion, patience, and love that my equine partners embody and model, every single day. In greeting my herd each day, I no longer ask, "What shall we do today?" and instead, am able to ask, "How shall we be together?" Because it's not about the doing to. It's all about being with.

It's not about the activity. It's all about relationships.

About the Author
Veronica Lac, PhD, LPC

Veronica Lac is the founder and executive director of The HERD Institute®, which offers training and certification for equine-facilitated psychotherapy and learning. She is also the founder and director of Share in The HERD, a non-profit organization that offers grants and scholarships for program development, training, and research in the equine-facilitated field. Veronica is passionate about increasing accessibility to and diversity of equine-facilitated services and providers and is committed to fostering collaboration within the field.

With 20 years of experience as a corporate trainer and mental health professional, and as a certified therapeutic riding instructor, Veronica brings an integrated perspective to equine-facilitated work. Her academic background includes a masters in training and performance management, a masters in Gestalt psychotherapy, and a PhD in psychology. She is trained in a number of modalities, including a mentorship in Adventures in Awareness with Barbara Rector, a pioneering influence in this field, and certification through the Gestalt Equine Institute of the Rockies. This has allowed her to combine her theoretical understanding with a relational and embodied approach to what she offers. Veronica is passionate about working with clients to enable them to reach their full potential, and is an experienced corporate trainer offering one-to-one coaching and organizational consultancy. Clients range from large corporate businesses to individuals, couples, and families. Veronica specializes in working with those who have eating disorders, trauma, and attachment issues and has developed equine- and canine-assisted programs for at-risk adolescents in collaboration with residential treatment centers and eating-disorder clinics.

Veronica is passionate about research in the field of equine-facilitated psychotherapy and has multiple publications internationally in peer-reviewed journals. In addition, she is on the executive boards of a number of professional organizations including: American Psychological Association, Division 32 (Secretary; University Professors Press (Editor); and The

Humanitarian Alliance. She is also a peer reviewer for *The Journal of Humanistic Psychology* and *The Humanistic Psychologist*.

Notes by Chapter

Chapter 2
[1] Beisser, A. (2004). The paradoxical theory of change. *International Gestalt Journal, 27*(2), 103–107.
[2] "The Greatest Showman, This is Me," 20th Century Fox, YouTube, 24 Dec. 2017. https://www.youtube.com/watch?v=XLFEvHWD_NE
[3] Zinker, J. (1978). *Creative process in gestalt therapy.* New York: First Vintage Books.

Chapter 3
[1] Lac, V. (2017). *Equine-facilitated psychotherapy and learning: The human–equine relational development (HERD) approach.* Cambridge, MA: Elsevier/Academic Press.
[2] Hallberg, L. (2008). *Walking the way of the horse: Exploring the power of the horse–human relationship* (p. 232). iUniverse, USA.
[3] Schlote, S. (2019). Personal communication.

Chapter 4
[1] Hallberg, L. (2008). *Walking the way of the horse: Exploring the power of the horse–human relationship.* iUniverse, USA.
[2] Buber, M. (1965). *Between man and man* (R.G. Smith, Trans.). New York, NY: Routledge Classics.
[3] Tolle, E. (1999). *The power of now: A guide to spiritual enlightenment.* Namaste Publishing.
[4] Merleau-Ponty, M. (2002). *Phenomenology of perceptions* (C. Smith, Trans.). New York, NY: Routledge.
[5] Safina, C. (2015). *Beyond words: What animals think and feel.* New York, NY: Henry Holt.
[6] Wohlleben, P. (2017). *The inner life of animals: Love, grief, and compassion—Surprising observations of a hidden world.* Berkeley, CA: Greystone Books.
[7] Foundation for Human Enrichment (2007). *Somatic Experiencing®– Healing Trauma* [training manual]. Boulder, CO: Somatic Experiencing® Trauma Institute.
[8] Buber, M. (1965). *Between man and man* (p. 11; R.G. Smith, Trans.). New York, NY: Routledge Classics..
[9] Frank, R. (2001). *Body of awareness: A somatic and developmental approach to psychotherapy* (p. 1). Cambridge, MA: Gestalt Press.
[10] Brown, B. (2012). *Daring greatly: How the courage to be vulnerable transforms the way we live, love, parent, and lead.* New York: Penguin Random House, LLC.

[11] Polster E., & Polster M. (1974). *Gestalt therapy integrated: Contours of theory &practice* (p. 99). New York, NY: Vintage Books.

[12] Bugental, J.F. T. (1978). *Psychotherapy and process: The fundamentals of an existential–humanistic approach* (p. 36). Reading, MA: Addison-Wesley.

Chapter 5

[1] Reber, D. (2018). *Differently wired: A parent's guide to raising an atypical child with confidence and hope.* New York, NY: Workmans Publishing Inc.

[2] Silberman, S. (2015). *NeuoTribes: The legacy of autism and the future of neurodiversity.* New York: Penguin Random House, LLC.

Chapter 6

[1] Yalom, I. D. (2001). *The gift of therapy: Reflections on being a therapist.* London, England: Piatkus Books. (Originally published 1980)

[2] Ad Council, (2020). "Love has no labels." ttps://www.adcouncil.org/Our-Campaigns/Family-Community/Diversity-Inclusion

[3] Lyengar, S. (2010, July). *The art of choosing.* [video file]. Retrieved from https://www.youtube.com/watch?v=lDq9-QxvsNU

[4] Cummings, D. (2018). *What is existential freedom?* Retrieved from https://dolancummings.com/2018/08/03/what-is-existential-freedom/

[5] May, R. (2009). *Man's search for himself.* New York, NY: W. W. Norton & Company, Inc.

[6] Brown, B. (2012). *Daring greatly: How the courage to be vulnerable transforms the way we live, love, parent, and lead* (p. 64). New York: Penguin Random House, LLC.

[7] Buettner, D. (2008). *The blue zones: 9 lessons for living longer from the people who've lived the longest.* Washington, DC: National Geographic Society.

[8] Frankl, V.E. (1959). *Man's search for meaning.* Boston, MA: Beacon Press.

[9] Rowlands, M. (2008). *The philosopher and the wolf: Lessons from the wild on love, death, and happiness,* London, UK: Granta Publications.

[10] Clance, P.R., & Imes, S. A. (1978). The imposter phenomenon in high achieving women: Dynamics and therapeutic interventions. *Psychotherapy: Theory, Research, and Practice, 15,* pp. 241–247

Chapter 7

[1] Ronseal. (2015). "Does exactly what it says on the tin." Retrieved from https://www.youtube.com/watch?v=OkGaq9xiQZY

[2] Bergum, V., & Dossetor, J. (2015). *Relational ethics: The full meaning of respect.* Hagerstown, MD: University Publishing Group.

[3] De Giorgio, F., & De Giorgio-Schoorl, J. (2017). *Equus Lost?: How we misunderstand the nature of the horse-human relationship—Plus*

brave new ideas for the future (pp. 32, 92, 113, 96). North Pomfret, VT: Trafalgar Square Books.

[4] Project Implicit (2011). Retrieved on January 20, 2020 from https://implicit.harvard.edu/implicit/

[5] Kepner, J. (1987). *Body process: A gestalt approach to working with the body in psychotherapy.* New York, NY: Gardner Press.

[6] Lac, V. (2017). Equine-facilitated psychotherapy and learning: The Human–Equine Relational Development (HERD) approach. Cambridge, MA: Elsevier/Academic Press.

[7] Buber, M. (1958). *I and Thou* (R.G. Smith, Trans.). New York, NY: Charles Scribner & Sons.

Chapter 8
[1] Zinker, J. (1978). *Creative process in gestalt therapy.* New York: First Vintage Books

Chapter 9
[1] Merleau-Ponty, M. (2002). *Phenomenology of perceptions* (C. Smith, Trans.). New York, NY: Routledge.

[2] Perls, F.S., Hefferline, R., & Goodman, P. (1977). *Gestalt therapy: Excitement and growth in the human personality.* New York, NY: Bantam Books.

Chapter 10
[1] Lewin, K. (1943). Defining the 'field at a given time.' *Psychological Review, 50*(3), pp. 292–310. https://doi.org/10.1037/h0062738